UNDERSTANDING FAITH
Understanding Islam

UNDERSTANDING FAITH

SERIES EDITOR: PROFESSOR FRANK WHALING

Also Available

Understanding the Baha'i Faith, *Wendi Momen with Moojan Momen*
Understanding Buddhism, *Perry Schmidt-Leukel*
Understanding Christianity, *Gilleasbuig Macmillan*
Understanding Islam, *Cafer S. Yaran*
Understanding Judaism, *Jeremy Rosen*
Understanding Sikhism, *Owen Cole*

Forthcoming

Understanding the Brahma Kumaris, *Frank Whaling*
Understanding Chinese Religions, *Xinzhong Yao*
Understanding Hinduism, *Frank Whaling*

UNDERSTANDING FAITH

SERIES EDITOR: PROFESSOR FRANK WHALING

Understanding Islam

Professor Cafer S. Yaran

Faculty of Theology
Istanbul University

DUNEDIN ACADEMIC PRESS
Edinburgh

Published by
Dunedin Academic Press Ltd
Hudson House
8 Albany Street
Edinburgh EH1 3QB
Scotland

ISBN 978-1-903765-30-2
ISSN 1744-5833

British Library Cataloguing in Publication Data
A catalogue record for this book is available from the British Library

Typeset by Makar Publishing Production
Printed in Great Britain by Cromwell Press

Contents

Preface

Islam is the world's second largest religion and the Islamic civilisation is one of the great civilisations in history. Islamic faith, ethics and spirituality guide about 1.3 billion Muslims, 25 million of whom live in the West, helping them to live a life of virtue and happiness both in this world and in the hereafter. In Western Europe, the number of immigrant Muslims lies somewhere between six and eight million. In countries like France and England, Islam has become the second most important religion. Islamic mystics or Sufis, like Ibn al-'Arabi and Rumi, have become a best-selling publishing phenomenon and they have provided valuable insights and inspiration, even to many contemporary non-Muslims, concerning divine love, religious tolerance and spiritual development.

However, Islam is also one of the most misunderstood religions, especially, indeed increasingly, today. A strange idea has become firmly lodged in the imagination of people across the world, namely that there is a clash between Islam and Western civilisation. For some people Islam is a religion of war and violence, while for others it is a religion of peace and harmony as the literal translation of Islam into English indicates. Similar alternative, monolithic and reductionist views or images have been put forward about Muslims, too. For some people all Muslims are terrorists and intolerant people, while for others it is impossible for a Muslim to be a terrorist nor can a terrorist be a Muslim. There are many other controversial issues about Islam and Muslims in our contemporary world. This highlights the urgent need for an academic and sympathetic understanding of Islam.

In its theological dimension the bedrock of Islam is the 'unity of God' or ethical monotheism based on the Qur'anic revelation. The motto of Muslims, as enunciated in the Qur'an, is 'the best in this world as well as the best in the Hereafter'. But numerous different approaches, understandings and forms of applications have been built on these foundations, ranging from the theological, philosophical and Sufic to the fundamentalist, traditionalist, modernist and postmodernist of recent times.

In this book, however, I will try to present Islam from a mainstream and moderate perspective rather than from a specific point of view. I use the concept of moderate here not only in its contemporary and controversial meaning restricted to political and social issues but rather in its perennial and more comprehensive meaning. For moderation is one of the most significant and respected values and virtues of Islamic religion, both in religious and ethical attitudes and also in worldly life. The Qur'an exhorts believers '... do not transgress. Assuredly, Allah does not love the transgressors' (5:87). Some Qur'anic verses relate this advice directly to religious issues: 'Commit no excess in your religion, nor say nothing but the truth about Allah' (4:171). And the Prophet Muhammad said in general that 'The golden mean is the best of things.'

Although some Muslims will not recognise my name, Cafer Sadık, when it is written using Turkish transliteration, it is actually the name of a well-known Muslim scholar, Ja'far as-Sadiq. After graduating from the Faculty of Theology (*İlahiyat Fakültesi*) in Turkey, I completed my doctorate in Philosophy of Religion at the Department of Theology, Religious Studies and Islamic Studies in Lampeter, UK. I now lecture on the Philosophy of Religion and Islamic Ethics at the Faculty of Theology of Istanbul University.

I am a Muslim by faith and a philosopher of religion by profession. Being Muslim necessitates being sympathetic and faithful to Islam, and being a philosopher means being as critical and objective as possible. I think this is an advantage when writing a book called *Understanding Islam*. To understand something is to be able to see it from a positive perspective, far removed from both unfair prejudices and polemics against it and also unaffected by exaggerated propaganda and politics in favour of it. I believe that to understand something depends more on the sincerity of your intentions and your perception of the object to be understood, rather than on whether you believe in it or belong to it. In theory, therefore, I believe that anyone who really wishes to understand Islam can, and I hope that this book will help them to do so.

1

Historical Dimension:
First Manifestation and Later Developments

The Arabic word 'Islam' simply means submission or obedience and derives from a word which literally means, among other things, peace and purity. As a religion Islam requires its followers to seek peace and happiness in this world and in the next through submission to the will of God, *Allah*, and obedience to His commands and recommendations. A Muslim is someone who obeys Allah in the way taught by the prophets, especially by the Prophet Muhammad. For Muslims, Islam is the name of the same universal truth that God revealed through all His prophets to every people, as well as the name of a specific religion revealed to the Prophet Muhammad.

THE MONOTHEISTIC TRADITION

For Muslims, the term *Islam* is not only the name of the specific religion revealed through the Prophet Muhammad, but also the common name of all the divine religions that God revealed through all His prophets to every people from Adam, the first prophet, to Muhammad, the last one. Although their proper names are different in various languages, the soul of all the divine religions is the same; and it is called Islam. The Qur'an uses the terms Islam and Muslim for the religions of all the prophets. The prophet Abraham, in particular, embodies the message of Islam and Muslim before the Prophet Muhammad in some Qur'anic verses: 'He has chosen you, and has not laid upon you in religion any hardship; the faith of your father Abraham. He named you Muslims previously, and in this [Scripture], that the Messenger may be a witness against you, and that you may be witnesses against all people' (22:78).

The nature of the original message and mission of all the prophets is the same. All of them called on the people to believe in and worship God alone, as well as believing in the Last Day and doing good deeds among their fellows. This common monotheistic ground is explained in the Qur'an, where it is stated that 'We did not send any Messenger before you, but that We revealed to him, 'there is no god but Me; therefore worship Me alone!'' (21:25).

As a verse in the Qur'an instructs us, as Muslims, 'We believe in Allah and that which is revealed to us and that which was revealed to Abraham and Ishmael and Isaac and Jacob and the tribes; and that which was vouchsafed to Moses and Jesus and the Prophets from their Lord. We make no distinction between any of them...' (3:84). We have to believe in the 25 prophets whose names are mentioned in the Qur'an. We also believe in the other prophets who, according to the Qur'an (35:24), have passed among every nation, and in all the prophets in general because the Qur'an talks about the existence of many messengers who are not mentioned in the Qur'an (4:164). Nevertheless, we are not in a position to be definite about a particular prophet outside the list of those actually named in the Qur'an.

The Qur'an's confirmation of the universality of revelation, however, does not mean that everything that passed as religion yesterday or does so today is completely authentic and that another prophet and revelation will not be sent. To use the terms of the Qur'an, God's 'mercy' towards humankind required the sending of many prophets, particularly before humanity had matured in many respects: '(O Muhammad) We have only sent you as a mercy for all worlds' (21:107).

THE PROPHET MUHAMMAD

Throughout history, whenever the divine principles were neglected or denied by the people for various religious, social or economic reasons and whenever there was an urgent need to renew the religious and moral life of society, God revealed these messages through another prophet. According to Muslims, God chose Muhammad as His last prophet and revealed the Holy Qur'an to him. The religion of Islam, in the narrower sense we know today, is based on divine revelation, the Qur'an, and the interpretation, application and additional sayings of the Prophet Muhammad. In this sense Islam is a religion that is based upon the holy book of the Qur'an revealed to the Prophet Muhammad by God; it insists on a world-view mainly based on the unity of God and on a way of life of ethical responsibility and accountability that cares for the other members of society, as well as personal spiritual improvement; moreover, it promises its adherents satisfaction in this world and salvation in the hereafter. As is well known, the concept of Muslim, in such a narrow sense, refers to someone who adheres to God's revelation in the Qur'an, as spoken by the Prophet Muhammad.

Religion and Society in Arabia before the Birth of the Prophet

The religion of Arabia was tribal polytheism and paganism. Gods and goddesses served as protectors of individual tribes, and their spirits were associated with sacred objects – trees, stones, springs, and wells. Mecca possessed a central shrine of the gods, the Kaaba, which housed the 360 idols of tribal patron deities and was the site of a great annual pilgrimage and fair. The Meccans did also possess the notion of the one high God, but they believed that idols had the power to intercede with Him. Curiously enough, they did not believe in the resurrection and afterlife. They saw no meaning or accountability beyond this life – no resurrection of the body, divine judgement, or eternal punishment or reward. Thus, Arabian religion had little sense of individual or communal moral responsibility.

Mecca was also the traditional centre of Arabian trade; it was the crossroads of trade routes between East and West, North and South. It had a city-state governed by a council of ten hereditary chiefs who enjoyed a clear division of powers. These tribal elders formed an advisory council within which the tribal chief exercised his leadership and authority as the first among equals. As well-reputed caravan leaders, the Meccans were able to obtain permission from neighbouring empires like Iran, Byzantium and Abyssinia to visit their countries and transact import and export business. The principal sources of livelihood were herding, agriculture, trade and raiding.

Although not much interested in preserving ideas and records in writing, they cultivated the arts and letters, like poetry, oratory discourses and folk tales. Tribal affiliation and law were the basis not only for identity but also for protection. The threat of family or group vendetta, the law of retaliation, was of vital importance in a society lacking a central political authority or law. Intertribal warfare was a long-established activity. Burying girls alive was practised in certain classes. In brief, the emergence of Mecca as a major mercantile centre, new wealth, the rise of a new commercial oligarchy, greater division between social classes, and a growing disparity between rich and poor strained the traditional system of tribal values and social security in the pre-Islamic period.

Birth and Early Life of the Prophet

It was in the midst of such conditions and into this environment that Muhammad was born. The exact date of his birth is disputed, but it is agreed to be around 570 CE. His father, Abdullah, had died before he was born, and it was his grandfather who took him in charge. According to the prevailing custom, the child was entrusted to a Bedouin foster mother, with whom he spent several years in the desert. When the child was brought back home, his mother, Aminah, took him to his maternal uncles at Medina to visit Abdullah's tomb. On the return journey, his mother died suddenly, leaving Muhammad who was said to be about six years old at the time. At Mecca, another bereavement awaited him since his affectionate grandfather died soon after. Having suffered such privations, at the age of eight he was placed in the care of his uncle, Abu Talib, whose love and protection persisted long after the Prophet proclaimed his mission and the new faith. He served as a shepherd boy to some neighbours and then, at the age of ten, he accompanied his uncle when he led a caravan to Syria.

By the time he was twenty-five, Muhammad had become well known in the city for the integrity of his disposition and the honesty of his character. An honourable and successful businesswoman, Khadijah, offered him employment and he was responsible for taking her goods for sale to Syria. Delighted with the unusual profits, she offered him her hand. The union proved happy. During their fifteen years of marriage, they enjoyed a very close relationship and had two sons and four daughters. The Prophet had a monogamous marriage until Khadijah died when he was fifty years old.

Beginning of Religious Consciousness and Revelation

Not much is known about the religious practices of the Prophet Muhammad until he was thirty-five years old, except that he had never worshipped idols and that he enjoyed great respect for his judgement and trustworthiness, as was reflected by his nickname al-Amin, the trusted one. It may be stated that there were a few others in Mecca, called *hanifs*, who had likewise revolted against the senseless practice of paganism, although remaining faithful to the Kaaba as the house dedicated to the one God by its builder Abraham. Muhammad was of a deeply religious nature and had long detested the decadence of his society. After he was thirty-five, Muhammad became more and more absorbed in spiritual meditations. Like his grandfather, he used to retire for the whole month of Ramadan to the Cave of Hira near the summit of Jabal al-Nur, the 'Mountain of Light' near Mecca.

He was forty years old and it was the fifth consecutive year since he started his annual retreats, when one night towards the end of the month of Ramadan, a heavenly intermediary, later identified by tradition as the angel Gabriel, commanded him to 'Read'. Muhammad responded that he had nothing to read. Twice the angel repeated the command, and each time a frightened and bewildered Muhammad pleaded that he did not know what to read. Finally, the first verses of the revelation that constitutes the beginning of Surah 96, 'The Clot', came to him: 'Read: In the name of your Lord who created, Created man from a clinging clot. Read: Your Lord is the Most Bountiful. Who taught by the pen. Taught man what he did not know' (96:1–5).

Deeply affected, he returned home and related to his wife what had happened, expressing his fears that it might have been something diabolic or the action of evil spirits. She consoled him, saying that he had always been a man of charity and generosity, helping the poor, the orphans, the widows and the needy, and assured him that God would protect him against all evil. Thus began his prophetic mission, which was to be carried out in the most difficult situation conceivable, for the message was one of uncompromising monotheism in a city that was the centre of Arabian idolatry.

The Mission at Mecca

The Prophet began by preaching his mission secretly first among his intimate friends, then among the members of his own tribe, and thereafter publicly in the city and suburbs. He insisted on belief in One Transcendent God, in resurrection and the Last Judgement. He invited men to charity and beneficence. At first only Khadijah, his cousin Ali ibn Abi Talib, and the Prophet's old friend Abu Bakr accepted the message that was revealed to him. Gradually, however, a number of others, including such eminent personalities as Umar ibn al-Khattab, who was later to become the second caliph after Abu Bakr, and Uthman ibn Affan, the future third caliph, embraced Islam. The very success of the Prophet's mission made the opposition to him and his followers more severe every day.

The number of his adherents increased gradually, but following his denunciation of paganism, the opposition also grew more intense as many rallied to defend their ancestral beliefs. For the powerful and prosperous Meccan oligarchy, Muhammad's monotheistic message, with its condemnation of the socioeconomic inequities of Meccan life, constituted a direct challenge not only to traditional polytheistic religion but also to the power and prestige of the establishment, threatening their economic, social and political interests. For the Prophet not only denounced false contracts, usury, and the neglect and exploitation of orphans and widows, but he also defended the rights of the poor and the oppressed, asserting that the rich had an obligation to them.

Meccan opposition escalated from derision and verbal attacks to physical torture of the Prophet and those who had embraced his religion. In despair the Prophet Muhammad advised his companions to leave their native town and take refuge abroad, in Abyssinia. When a large number of the Meccan Muslims migrated to Abyssinia, the leaders of the city decided on a complete boycott of the tribe of the Prophet: nobody was to talk to them or have commercial or matrimonial relations with them. The boycott caused stark misery among the innocent victims, who included children, the old and the sick. After three dire years, the boycott was lifted, but the Prophet's wife and Abu Talib, the chief of the tribe and his uncle, died soon after because of the privations they had suffered.

Migration to Medina

The annual pilgrimage of the Kaaba brought to Mecca people from all parts of Arabia. The Prophet Muhammad tried to persuade one tribe after another to offer him shelter and allow him to carry on with his mission. Finally, he met half a dozen inhabitants of Medina. They embraced Islam, promising to provide additional adherents and the necessary help from Medina. The following year a dozen new Medinans took the oath of allegiance to him and asked him to provide a missionary teacher. The work of the missionary Mus'ab proved very successful and he led a contingent of seventy-three new converts to Mecca at the time of the pilgrimage. The converts invited the Prophet and his Meccan companions to migrate to their town and promised to shelter the Prophet and to treat him and his companions as their own kith and kin. Secretly, and in small groups, the greater part of the Muslims emigrated to Medina. Later the Prophet Muhammad also left Mecca secretly in the company of Abu-Bakr, his faithful friend. After several incidents, they succeeded in reaching Medina in safety. This happened in 622. This migration *(hijra)* marked a turning point in the Prophet's fortunes and a new stage in the history of the Islamic movement.

In Medina, he invited representatives of both the Muslims and non-Muslim inhabitants of the region and suggested the establishment of a city-state. With their assent, he endowed the city with a written constitution in which he defined the duties and rights both of the citizens and the head of state, the Prophet Muhammad. However, concern for the material interests of the community never led to neglect of the spiritual aspects. Hardly a year had passed after the migration to Medina, when the most rigorous of spiritual disciplines, the obligation to fast for the whole month of Ramadan every year, was imposed on every adult Muslim man and woman.

Wars and the Occupation of Mecca

In Medina the nascent community was immediately attacked by the Meccans. The Meccans sent an ultimatum to the Medinans demanding the surrender or at least the expulsion of Muhammad and his companions. Several important battles then took place between the Muslims in Medina and the Meccan polytheists, in which the Muslims prevailed, usually against unbelievable odds. In 624 at Badr, near Medina, the Muslim forces, though greatly outnumbered, defeated the Meccan army. After a year of preparation, in 625 the Meccans again invaded Medina to avenge their defeat at Badr. They were now four times as numerous as the Muslims. After a bloody encounter at Uhud, the enemy retired and the issue remained undecided. In 627, frustrated by Muhammad's growing strength, the Meccans mounted an all-out siege of Medina in order to crush the Muslims once and for all. At the 'Battle of the Ditch', the Muslims held out so successfully against a coalition of Meccans and mercenary Bedouins that the coalition disintegrated and the Meccans withdrew.

In 630 the Muslims marched on Mecca, ten thousand strong. The Meccans capitulated. Eschewing vengeance and the plunder of conquest, the Prophet instead accepted a settlement, granting an amnesty rather than wielding the sword against his former enemies. For their part, the Meccans converted to Islam, accepted Muhammad's leadership and were incorporated within the *Ummah*. Muhammad purified the Kaaba of the idols inside and on top of it and then, along with other rites, performed circumambulations of the House of God, following the footsteps of Abraham. This pilgrimage is called *hajj* and to this day it continues to be one of the 'pillars' or fundamental elements of Islam. However, Muhammad did not remain in the city of his birth and upbringing. Instead, he returned to Medina.

Farewell Sermon and the Death of the Prophet

In 632, when the Prophet went to Mecca for *hajj* (pilgrimage), he met 140,000 Muslims there, who had come from different parts of Arabia to fulfil their religious obligation. He addressed them in his celebrated farewell sermon, in which he gave a resume of his teachings: belief in One God without images or symbols; the equality of all believers without distinctions of race or class, the superiority of individuals being based solely on piety; the sanctity of life, property and honour; the abolition of interest, vendettas and private justice; better treatment of women; the obligatory inheritance and distribution of the property of deceased persons among near relatives of both sexes, and removal of the possibility of wealth accumulating in the hands of the few. The Qur'an and the conduct of the Prophet were to serve as the bases of law and a healthy criterion for every aspect of human life.

On his return to Medina, Muhammad fell ill and a few weeks later he breathed his last. When he died in June 632, all Arabia was united under the banner of Islam.

Muhammad, the Seal of the Prophets

The prophet of Islam is exemplary precisely because he is a man–prophet. The Qur'an emphasises again and again that he is a man like any other, except to the extent that the angel Gabriel brought him revelation. He was also given the most exalted and noble character, and he was chosen as a model for Muslims to emulate as mentioned in the verse: 'Verily in the messenger of Allah you have a good example for him who hopes for Allah and the Last Day, and has remembered Allah much' (33:21).

To comprehend the significance of the Prophet Muhammad in Islam, it is necessary to remember that the great prophets or founders of religions are of two types. The first is exemplified by Jesus, and the second is exemplified by Moses, David and Solomon in the Abrahamic world, and by Rama and Krishna in Hinduism. These Hebrew prophets, as well as some avataric figures from Hinduism, were also political leaders and rulers of a community. They were married and had children. The Prophet Muhammad must be seen as belonging to this second category. His contemplation was inward, while outwardly he had to face nearly every possible human situation (Nasr, 2002:33–4). He served as both religious and political head of Medina: prophet of God, ruler, military commander, chief judge and lawgiver.

The Prophet Muhammad is sometimes criticised by some non-Muslims for his military activities and his marriages. For Muslims, Muhammad provides the ideal model of a prophet, who leads his people by example and demonstrates in person how life should be lived in the world. Since life on this earth will always be subject to conflict, it is essential to have an example of the best ethical conduct of war and politics. Likewise, since human life requires procreation and the family, there must be a religious model in this area as well.

In addition to this, one must remember that Muhammad's 'use of warfare in general was alien neither to Arab custom nor to that of the Hebrew prophets. Both believed that God had sanctioned battle with the enemies of the Lord. Biblical stories about the exploits of kings and prophets such as Moses, Joshua, Elijah, Samuel, Jehu, Saul, and David recount the struggles of a community called by God and the permissibility, indeed requirement, to take up arms when necessary against those who had defied God' (Esposito, 1991:17). As a matter of fact, almost all Muhammad's wars were wars of defence not assault. In all the 'wars', extending over a period of ten years, the non-Muslims lost only about 250 persons on the battlefield, and the Muslims lost even fewer. By making relatively few incisions, the whole continent of Arabia, covering over a million square miles, was cured of the abscess of anarchy and immorality. By the end of these ten years of disinterested struggle, all the peoples of the Arabian Peninsula and the southern regions of Iraq and Palestine had voluntarily embraced Islam. Some Christian, Jewish and Parsi groups remained attached to their creeds and they were granted liberty of conscience, as well as judicial and juridical autonomy (Hamidullah, 1980:18–19).

When it comes to his marriages, it should be remembered that the Prophet had a monogamous marriage until his first wife, Khadijah, died when he was fifty years old. It was only in the last years of his life that he contracted other marriages, mostly for the political purpose of unifying the various tribes of Arabia. In fact, it is much better to quote from Esposito on this issue:

> In addressing the issue of Muhammad's polygynous marriages, it is important to remember several points. First, Semitic culture in general and Arab practice in particular permitted polygyny. It was common practice in Arabian society, especially among nobles and leaders. Though less common, polygyny was also permitted in biblical and even in postbiblical Judaism. From Abraham, David, and Solomon down to the reformation period, polygyny was practiced by some Jews. While Jewish law changed after the Middle Ages due to the influence of Christian rule, for Jews under Islamic rule, polygyny remained licit, though it was not extensively practiced. Second, during the prime of his life, Muhammad remained married to one woman, Khadija. Third, it was only after her death that he took a number of wives. Fourth, Muhammad's use of the special dispensation from God to exceed the limit of four wives imposed by the Qur'an, occurred only after the death of Khadija. Moreover, most of the eleven marriages had political and social motives. As was customary for Arab chiefs, many were political marriages to cement alliances. Others were marriages to the widows of his companions who had fallen in combat and were in need of protection. Remarriage was difficult in a society that emphasized virgin marriages. Aisha was the only

virgin that Muhammad married and the wife with whom he had the closest relationship. Fifth, as we shall see later, Muhammad's teachings and actions, as well as the Qur'anic message, improved the status of all women—wives, daughters, mothers, widows, and orphans.

Talk of the political and social motives behind many of the Prophet's marriages should not obscure the fact that Muhammad was attracted to women and enjoyed his wives. To deny this would contradict the Islamic outlook on marriage and sexuality, found in both revelation and Prophetic traditions, which emphasizes the importance of family and views sex as a gift from God to be enjoyed within the bonds of marriage. The many stories about Muhammad's concern and care for his wives reflect these values (Esposito, 1991:18–19).

As a result, the practice of the Prophet, his *Sunnah* or example, became the norm for Muslim personal and community life. Muslims observed and remembered stories about what the Prophet said and did. These reports or traditions, known as *hadith*, were preserved and passed on in oral and written form. The corpus of hadith literature reveals the comprehensive scope of Muhammad's example; for he is God's final Messenger, the 'Seal of Prophets', for Muslims as well as the exemplary human being. His greatest miracle was the Qur'anic revelation.

THE QUR'ANIC REVELATION

Qur'an literally means reading or recitation. While dictating this to his disciples, the Prophet Muhammad assured them it was the Divine revelation that had come to him. So, for Muslims, the Qur'an is the Book of God with no input from Muhammad. It is the literal word of God sent down from heaven, revealed one final time to the Prophet Muhammad as 'guidance for mankind, (a book of) clear proofs of guidance and the criterion (distinguishing right from wrong)' (Qur'an, 2:185). All Muslims, no matter which school they belong to, consider it as the verbatim revelation of God's Word made to descend into the heart, soul and mind of the Prophet of Islam through the agency of the archangel of revelation, Gabriel, or Jibra'il in Arabic. Muslims believe that the Messenger Muhammad is only an intermediary for the reception and communications of the revelations; he is neither author nor compiler.

The revelations came to the Prophet in fragments, from time to time. As soon as he received one, he used to communicate it to his disciples and ask them not only to learn it by heart but also to write it down and make multiple copies. In any case, for Muslims themselves, there is but a single text of the Qur'an consisting of 114 chapters of over 6,000 verses revealed to the

Prophet of Islam in Mecca and Medina over the twenty-three years of his prophetic mission. The order of the chapters of the Qur'an was also given by the Prophet through Divine inspiration.

The Qur'an is regarded by Muslims as the main miracle accomplished by the Prophet. By virtue of its claim of divine origin, the Qur'an has challenged men and *jinn* together to produce even a few verses equal to those of the Qur'an: 'Say: "If all men and jinn gathered together to produce the like of this Qur'an they could not produce one like it, though they were helpers one of another"' (17:88). The challenge has remained unanswered to this day.

During the caliphate of the third caliph, Uthman, some twenty years after the death of the Prophet, as many of those who had memorised the Qur'an were dying in various battles, the complete text of the Qur'an was copied in several manuscripts and sent to the four corners of the Islamic world. Later copies are based on this early definitive collection.

The Qur'an contains several grand themes. First of all, it deals with the Divine reality and many other theological issues. The core theological doctrines of Islam are summarised in the fourth chapter of the Qur'an: 'O you who believe! Believe in Allah and His Messenger and the Scripture which He has revealed to His Messenger, and the Scripture which He revealed before (you). Whoever disbelieves in Allah and His Angels and His Scriptures and His Messengers and the Last Day, he assuredly has gone far astray' (4:136). Second, the Qur'an says much about the natural world. The universe is the creature of God and everything in the world reflects the signs of God's power and mercy. Third, the Qur'an contains many pages on sacred history, but the episodes of this history are recounted more for their significance as lessons for the inner life of the soul than as historical accounts of ages past. The Qur'an also deals with laws for the individual and society. Furthermore, the Qur'an comes back again and again to the question of ethics, of good and evil, of the significance of living a virtuous life. Finally, the Qur'an speaks about eschatological events, about the end of this world, about the Day of Judgement, punishments and rewards: 'Whoever Works righteousness, man or woman, and has faith, We shall assuredly give him to live a goodly life, and We will bestow upon them their reward according to the best of what they used to do' (16:97).

The central factor in the creation of unity among Muslims is the Qur'an. For all Muslims, it is the very Word of God, with the same text and the same message for all Muslims, although interpretations of that message differ among various Muslim groups and there are levels of meaning to the text. The Qur'an is often succinct; it is in the practice of the Prophet that one must look for the method of application, the details and necessary explanations. The narrations on the Prophet Muhammad are called *hadith*, whether they concern what he said or did, or even what he simply tolerated among his disciples if they said or did something in his presence. The Qur'an reminds Muslims many times of the juridical importance of the hadith: 'O you who believe! Obey Allah and obey the Messenger...' (4:59); 'Whatever the Messenger gives you, accept it; and whatever he forbids you, abstain from it' (59:7); 'Verily in the Messenger of Allah you have a good example for him who hopes for Allah and the Last day, and has remembered Allah much' (33:21). For Muslims throughout the centuries, the messages of the Qur'an and the example of the Prophet Muhammad have constituted the formative and enduring foundation of Islamic faith and the Muslim way of life. They have served as the basic sources of Islamic culture and civilisation.

SOME BASIC CHARACTERISTICS OF ISLAM

There can be no doubt that the essence of Islam is *tawhid*, the act of affirming Allah to be the One, absolute, transcendent Creator, Lord and Master of all that is. Traditionally and simply expressed, *tawhid* is the conviction and witnessing that 'there is no God but God'. This negative statement, brief to the utmost limits of brevity, carries the greatest and richest meanings in the whole of Islam. *Tawhid* is that which gives Islamic faith and civilisation its identity, which binds all its constituents together and makes them an integral, organic body.

Another feature of Islam is that it does not divide life into watertight compartments of matter and spirit. It is well known that the motto of Islam is summed up in the expression of the Qur'an, 'Lord! Give us what is good in this world and in the Hereafter' (2:201). Islam will certainly not satisfy the extremists of either school, the ultra-spiritualists and the ultra-materialists, yet it can be practised by an overwhelming majority of people, who follow an intermediate path and seek to develop the body and the soul simultaneously, creating a harmonious equilibrium in the individual as a whole. Islam has insisted on the importance of both these constituents of humankind, and on their inseparability, so that one should not be sacrificed for the benefit of the other.

Islam aims at establishing equilibrium between these two aspects of life – the material and the spiritual. Its supreme achievement is the complete coordination of the spiritual and the material aspects of human life. In the teachings of Islam, both these aspects are not only reconciled to each other, in the sense of leaving no inherent conflict between man's bodily and moral existence, but the fact of their coexistence and actual inseparability is insisted upon as the natural basis of life. Indeed, the Qur'an recommends: 'Seek the abode of the Hereafter in that which Allah has given to you, and forget not your portion of the world' (28:77).

Islam lays very strong emphasis on the fact that man is composed simultaneously of two elements: body and soul; and that he (or she, of course) should not neglect either of these for the sole profit of the other. To devote oneself exclusively to spiritual needs would be to aspire to become an angel; to dedicate oneself to purely material needs would be to be degraded to the condition of a beast or plant, if not a devil. The aim of God's creation of man with a dual capacity remains unfulfilled if he does not maintain a harmonious equilibrium between the requirements of the body and those of the soul, simultaneously.

A corollary perhaps of the same all-embracing or bipolar conception of life is the fact that the Qur'an often uses the double formula, 'believe and do good works' (103:3); the mere profession of faith, without application or practice, does not have much value. Islam insists as much on the one as on the other. Another frequently used exhortation to 'perform *salat* [prayer] and give *zakat* [almsgiving]' is only a specific form of the more general bipolar formula, 'believe and do good works', which can be regarded as the fundamental form of the Qur'an's religious, moral and social commandments.

The bipolarity of Islam is evident in many other ways. In Islamic theology, for instance, God is not only transcendent and non-material, beyond any physical perception (cf. Qur'an 6:103: 'Vision comprehends Him not'), but He is also immanent and omnipresent (cf. Qur'an 50:16: 'We are nearer to him than his jugular vein'). In Islamic law and ethics, too, one can see both retaliation and forgiveness. The Qur'an makes a 'molecule' from these 'atoms': 'The recompense of an ill-deed is an ill-deed like thereof. But whosoever pardons and seeks reconciliation, his reward is with Allah' (42:40).

Another dimension of this conception is that Islam seeks to establish a balance between individualism and collectivism. It believes in the individual personality of man and holds everyone personally accountable to God. According to the Qur'an, 'Allah does not charge a soul with more than what it can bear. It shall be requited for whatever good and whatever evil it has done' (2:286). On the other hand, it also awakens a sense of social responsibility in man and enjoins the individual to subscribe to the social good. Islam neither neglects the individual nor society; it establishes a harmony and a balance between the two and assigns to each its proper due. In short, the most outstanding characteristic of Islam is that it establishes a unique harmony between body and soul, between heart and brain, between reason and intuition, between work and worship, between the individual and society, between permanence and change, between this world and the hereafter.

The teachings of Islam are simple and intelligible. The unity of God, the prophethood of Muhammad and the concept of life-after-death are the basic articles of its faith. Its message is for the entire human race and the Prophet is a Messenger for the whole of humanity. In the words of the Qur'an: '(O Muhammad) We have only sent you as a mercy for all worlds' (21:107). In Islam all men are equal, whatever their colour, language, race or nationality. Islam addresses itself to the conscience of humanity and banishes all false barriers of race, status and wealth. It awakens in man the faculty of reason and exhorts him to use his intellect. It enjoins him to see things in the light of reality. The Qur'an advises man to pray: 'My Lord! Increase me in knowledge!' (20:114).

The traditional religious life of a Muslim is also based on a rhythmic movement between two poles, the poles of transcendence and immanence, of rigour and compassion, of justice and forgiveness, of the fear of punishment and the hope for mercy based on God's love for us. Muslims see themselves as the 'middle community' in the world on the basis of the famous Qur'anic verse in which Muslims are addressed as follows: 'Thus have We made you a middle nation (*Ummah*), so that you may be witnesses against mankind' (2:143). This verse can be and in fact has been understood in many ways. On a theological level, Islam came to emphasise the middle ground, to strike a balance between this world and the next. Another interpretation, which is primarily ethical, is that 'middle nation' means that God chose for Muslims the golden mean, the avoidance of extremes in ethical and religious actions.

Muslims regard themselves as responsible for all happenings around them; and they strive for the establishment of right and the abolition of wrong on every occasion and in every direction in accordance with the verse of the Qur'an: 'You are the best community that has been raised up for mankind. You enjoin what is good and forbid what is evil' (3:110). However, they have to avoid all kinds of extremism. For extremism in religious matters is criticised and banned both by the Qur'an and by the Prophet Muhammad. It is said in the Qur'an that, 'O you who believe! ... do not transgress. Assuredly, Allah does not love the transgressors' (5:87).

In the time of the Prophet Muhammad, Abu Dharr, Salman, Abu'd-Darda and some of his other companions who liked asceticism, did not obtain permission from the Prophet to lead, for instance, lives of recluses, to fast perpetually and to be castrated in horror of carnal pleasures. On the contrary, the Prophet encouraged them to marry and added, 'You have obligations even with regard to your own body' (al-Bukhari). It had so happened that one of the Prophet's companions came to see him dressed in miserable attire, even though he was a well-to-do person. When the Prophet asked him the reason, he replied that he preferred to look wretched, not out of miserliness but out of piety because he wished to put the needy before himself. The Prophet did not approve of this and set a limit to self-sacrifice; he ordered: 'When God has given you means, the traces of His bounty should be visible on you' (at-Tirmidhi).

According to a modern Muslim scholar, al-Faruqi, surrounding the centre of Qur'anic ideas about God and His relevance to creation is a body of methodological principles governing man's response to divinity. Taken as a whole, these principles or characteristics establish a world-view constituted as follows:

1. Rationalism or the subjection of all knowledge, including religious knowledge, to the dictates of reason and common sense, the repudiation of myth, of paradox, of ultimately contradictory

positions, acquiescence to proof and evidence, and openness to further evidence and readiness to alter one's knowledge and attitude according to the demands of new evidence.

2. Humanism, or the doctrine, first, that all humans are born innocent, there being neither original sin nor guilt; second, that they are free to determine their individual destinies since neither matter nor social order can or should restrict their movement or efforts to order their lives in accordance with the best dictates of their own consciences; third, that they are equal before God and the law since no discrimination is legitimate that bases itself upon race, colour, language, inherited culture, religion, or inherited social position; fourth, that they are all by nature capable of making judgements of truth and falsehood, of good and evil, of desirableness and its opposite, since without such capacity for judgement and action, neither humanity nor moral merit nor demerit are possible; fifth, that they are all responsible, certain to be accountable and will receive from their Creator, whether in this world or the next, exactly what their deeds have earned for them.

3. World- and life-affirmation, or the doctrine that God created life to be lived and not denied or destroyed, and the world to be enjoyed; that Creation is subservient to man, malleable and transformable by him according to his wishes and design; that both life and the world are to be promoted and developed, culture and civilization to be nurtured and to issue in human self-realization in knowledge, in *taqwa* and *ihsan* (piety and righteousness), and in beauty.

4. Societism, or the doctrine that man's cosmic value lies in his membership in and contribution to human society; that his individual self is certainly an end-in-itself; yet more enobled, and hence conditioned, by its subjection to humanity as an end-in-itself (Al-Faruqi, 1986:109–10).

These basic Islamic characteristics and principles based on the Qur'anic essence have created the history and culture of Islamic community as well as Islamic faith, ritual, ethics and spirituality.

A BRIEF HISTORY OF THE ISLAMIC COMMUNITY

A Brief History

During the period of the Prophet Muhammad and the first four caliphs of Islam (632–661), the spread of Islam and the conquest of Arabia were completed and Islamic rule was extended throughout much of the Middle East and North Africa.

Among the reasons for the rapid and peaceful spread of Islam was the simplicity of its doctrine. It calls for faith in only One God worthy of worship.

It also repeatedly instructs man to use his powers of intelligence and observation. Much of its expansion throughout history was also the result of the activities of merchants, traders and mystics, as well as soldiers, who proved effective missionaries in carrying the message of Islam.

In successive centuries, two great caliphates, the Umayyad (661–750) in Damascus and the Abbasid (749–1258) in Baghdad, oversaw the expansion of the Islamic empire as a world political force and the consolidation of Islamic civilisation.

After the destruction of the Abbasid Empire, from the thirteenth to the eighteenth century the Islamic world consisted of a string of local states and sultanates. Among the most powerful sultanates or empires were the Ottoman Empire in Turkey and much of the Arab world and Eastern Europe, the Safavid Empire in Persia, and the Mughal Empire in the Indian subcontinent.

From the eighteenth to the twentieth centuries the Islamic world witnessed a period of upheaval and renewal. Muslims struggled with the failures of their societies and the impact of European colonialism, and they responded to the intellectual and moral challenges of a changing modern world.

In the nineteenth century, a series of revivalist movements rose up across much of the Muslim world. These shared a common concern for the decline of Muslim fortunes and a common conviction that the cure was a purification of their societies and way of life by a more faithful return to pristine Islam.

In the late nineteenth and early twentieth centuries, Islamic modernist movements responded to the intellectual and political challenge of Western hegemony. Maintaining that Islam and modernity, revelation and reason were compatible, the modernist scholars and thinkers advocated religious, legal, educational and social reforms to revitalise the Muslim community.

Islamic modernism, however, remained attractive primarily to an intellectual elite. This limitation contributed to the emergence of some revivalist or so-called fundamentalist movements, which criticised modernist reformers for westernising Islam. Instead they proclaimed the self-sufficiency of Islam as a response to the demands of modern life, and they tried to implement an Islamic system of government and law through social and political action, especially during the 1970s and 1980s.

In the 1990s Islamic revivalism ceased to be restricted to small, marginal organisations on the periphery of society but instead became part of mainstream Muslim society, producing a new class of modern, educated, but Islamically oriented elites who work alongside their secular counterparts.

As in the past Islam continues to be a dynamic religious tradition, facing new problems and issues, but also providing guidance for almost one-fifth of the world's population (Esposito, 1995:247–54).

Sectarianism: Sunni and Shi'i Islam

The issue of leadership after the death of Muhammad led to a major split in the Muslim community and gave rise to its two major sects: the Sunni, who today represent about 87 per cent of the world's Muslims, and the Shi'i, who constitute 13 per cent. The Sunni majority believe that Muhammad died without designating a successor. Thus, the elders of the community selected a caliph to be political leader. The Shi'i minority believe that Muhammad did in fact designate the senior male of his family, Ali ibn Abi Talib, to lead the community.

The word *sunni* in Arabic comes from the term *ahl al-sunnah wa'l-jama'ah*, that is the people who follow the *Sunnah* of the Prophet and the majority, while Shi'ism comes from the Arabic term *shi'at 'Ali*, meaning partisans of Ali ibn Abi Talib.

The Schools of Theology

In Islam theology is called *'ilm al-kalam* or simply *kalam*. First of all, in the Sunni world of the eighth century the Mu'tazilite school developed, which favoured extensive use of reason in the interpretation of religious matters. In the tenth century a new school of *kalam* called the Ash'arite arose in Baghdad with the aim of creating a middle ground on many questions, such as the use of reason in religious matters. Ash'arism, which many orientalists have identified with Islamic theological orthodoxy as such, spread quickly among the Shafi'i school of law and reached its peak in many ways with al-Ghazali, who did, however, hold some non-Ash'arite views, and with Fakhr al-Din al-Razi, in the eleventh and twelfth centuries. Gradually Ash'arism spread among the Hanafi and Maliki schools of law as well and became the most widely held school of *kalam* in the Sunni world until the contemporary period. But there were also other Sunni schools of *kalam* that held sway in certain localities, such as Maturidism in Khurasan and Central Asia and Tahawism in Egypt.

The Schools of Law or Jurisprudence

As far as Sunni Islam is concerned, its followers are divided according to the *madhab*s or schools of law they follow. In the eighth and ninth centuries the schools of jurisprudence were codified by the doctors of the law. Some of the schools died out, but four have survived during the past millennium and constitute the main body of traditional Sunnism. They are the Hanafi, Maliki, Shafi'i, and Hanbali schools of law.

Sufism or Islamic Mysticism

The development of Islamic law was paralleled in the eighth and ninth centuries by another movement, Sufism. It focuses more on an interior spiritual life of personal piety, morality and the devotional love of God. By the twelfth century, what had been primarily circles of spiritual elites were transformed into a mass, popular movement.

From the eleventh and twelfth centuries onwards, Sufism became organised in orders, usually named after their founders; older ones, such as

Rifa'iyyah and Qadiriyyah, which still survive, were followed by many more recent ones, such as the Shadhiliyyah, the Khalwatiyyah, the Mawlawiyyah, the Chishtiyyah, the Naqshbandiyyah and the Ni'matullahiyyah. Some of the orders have died out over time and occasionally new ones are created, but they all rely on the continuity of the 'initiatic' chain, or *silsilah*, which goes back to the Prophet. There is hardly an Islamic country in which Sufi orders are not to be found, and since the early twentieth century some orders, beginning with the Shadhiliyyah, have spread into Europe and America.

Islamic Philosophy

The history of Islamic philosophy dates back to the first part of the ninth century. Before that philosophical activity consisted of translation from Greek or Syriac, as well as peripheral incursions into the field of philo sophical composition. The author who inaugurated the whole tradition of genuine philosophical writing was Abu Yusuf Ya'qub al-Kindi (d. *c*.866)

Al-Kindi made the first major attempt to harmonise philosophy with Islamic religion. He did not believe that there was a conflict between philo sophy and revelation. Despite his dependence on Aristotle, al-Kindi did not confine the function of philosophy to purely abstract thought; instead, he believed philosophy to be the 'handmaid' of religion. For the truth the philosophers seek is not different from the truth to which the prophets have summoned humankind. Al-Kindi states in his thesis that the One is the originator of everything, not in the manner of emanation adumbrated by the Neoplatonist philosophers but rather in the manner of creation *ex nihilo* laid down in the Qur'an. His eclectic work contained both Aristotelian and Neoplatonic elements and his philosophy tried to reconcile philosophical metaphysics with Islamic doctrines, which were developed by al-Farabi (*c*.870–950).

The first truly systematic philosopher of Islam was al-Farabi, who laid down the foundations of Islamic Neoplatonism. The three areas in which al-Farabi excelled were logic, political philosophy and metaphysics. The substance of al-Farabi's philosophy is contained in his best-known work *al-Madinah al-Fadilah* ('The Virtuous City'). This work provides a general outline of the universe at large, the mode of its emanation from the First Being and finally the virtuous mode of political association and the ultimate destiny of the soul. Al-Farabi identified the 'One' of Plotinus with the Islamic Allah and described a hierarchy in which all other things emanated by a neces sity of nature from this First Being, beginning with the First Intellect and proceeding through a series of nine other intellects. With the tenth intellect, which governs the sublunary world, the series of intellects is complete and the stage is set for the rise of the generable-corruptible entities of the lower world. The order of their generation is the reverse order of ascent from the lowest, the four elements, to the highest grade of becoming, human beings. The ultimate goal of a human being is happiness. However, the individual cannot attain happiness outside society, especially outside the 'virtuous city'. The virtuous city stands out as a moral and theoretical model, in so far as its inhabitants have apprehended the truth about God and the Afterlife, and live according to the precepts of virtue. Al-Farabi held that only the soul survived in an individual and, further, that only the souls of thinkers survived because 'undeveloped' minds were destroyed at death.

Neoplatonism in Islamic philosophy perhaps reached its climax in the thought of Ibn Sina (Avicenna, 980–1037). He developed the fundamental Neoplatonic themes outlined by his predecessor, al-Farabi, with the exception of politics. Ibn Sina, like al-Farabi, regarded the world as an emanation from the Necessary Being. In other words, he upheld the doctrine of the eternity of the world against the orthodox dogma of creation. Moreover, in the framework of the Greek theories of Aristotle and Plotinus, it was impossible that the Necessary Being should know particulars: he could have cognisance only of universals since cognition of the particular would introduce change in the Divine Mind, both in the sense of a temporal succession and a change of different objects. Ibn Sina also held that all human souls survived, since the body could not be resurrected, although he allowed that souls, after being separated from their bodies, especially those that were 'undeveloped' but morally virtuous, felt a kind of 'physical' pleasure since they were incapable of experiencing purely mental states. But in general he taught that the resurrection of the body was an imaginative myth with which the minds of the prophets were inspired in order to influence the moral character of the unthinking masses.

For the Neoplatonist or peripatetic Muslim philosophers like al-Farabi and Ibn Sina, religious truth was similar to rational or philosophical truth, but instead of being expressed in nakedly rational formulas, it manifested itself in imaginative symbols. This fact was responsible for its widespread acceptance by and effectiveness among the masses. Thus, religion was but philosophy for the masses, and its primary function was their moral education and purification. Thus, instead of saying, 'If you pursue moral good, your mind shall attain the real spiritual freedom which is bliss,' the Prophet said, 'If you are virtuous and perform these specific acts, you shall enter Paradise and will be saved from the flames of Hell' (Rahman, 1966:120).

Together with al-Farabi, Ibn Sina was devastatingly attacked by Abu Hamid al-Ghazali (1058–1111) in the work *Tahafut al-Falasifah* ('The Incoherence of the Philosophers'). Al-Ghazali elaborated 20 propositions against which the careless believer was to be on his guard. The three most pernicious issues for which the philosophers should be anathematised or be declared infidels (*takfir*) are, he stated, the eternity of the world; God's knowledge of universals, but not of particulars; and the denial of the resurrection of the body. For al-Ghazali, the world was deliberately created by God and did not just emanate, in Neoplatonic fashion, from a First Being. The doctrine of the eternity of the world was shown to be impossible, even rationally, apart from the fact that it denied the God of creative activity, in the real sense of the word. For the philosophical doctrine of the necessary emanation of the world from God was substituted God's voluntary activity. The rational constitution of God, operating by an inherent rational necessity, was replaced by the concept of the Will of God. God's knowledge of particulars was advocated both rationally and theologically. Similarly, the purely spiritual character of the philosophers' eschatology was rejected, asserting the resurrection of the body as well. But the most crucial basis of orthodox dissatisfaction with the philosophers' religion concerned the nature of religion and revelation itself. The character of the revelation, seen by the philosophers as being essentially intellectual, and especially the idea that religion is but a symbolic form of this intellectual truth, was resolutely rejected.

Al-Ghazali tells us in his autobiography that the study of philosophy, theology and esoteric doctrine did not quench his thirst for truth, and after years of study, teaching and reflection, he came to the conclusion that the Sufi route is the straightest route and their character is the best character. After al-Ghazali, the increasing aridity of medieval Muslim thought produced a reaction among many Muslims who began to yearn for a more personal communion with God than was possible in orthodox Islam with its prevailing philosophical systems. The result was Sufism or Islamic mysticism. Soon after the death of al-Ghazali, who had tried to reconcile Islamic sciences and Sufism, the first great organised Sufi orders began to appear at a popular level.

After al-Ghazali, a mystical element invaded philosophy as well, and produced what might be termed the *Ishraqi* (Illuminationist) school of Islamic philosophers. Its best-known exponent was al-Suhrawardi (1155–1191), whose thought was bound up with the science and nature of light. Light permeated everything and he envisaged a hierarchy of pure lights at the top of which stood the Light of Lights whose principle attribute was unity.

Aristotle's greatest Muslim disciple Ibn Rushd (Averroës, 1126–1198) has a unique place in the history of Islamic philosophy. He shows how his philosophical predecessors, al-Farabi and Ibn Sina, departed from Aristotle's thought. Furthermore, just as al-Ghazali attacked al-Farabi and Ibn Sina in *Tahafut al-Falasifah*, so Ibn Rushd in turn attacked al-Ghazali in his most famous work *Tahafut al-Tahafut* ('The Incoherence of the Incoherence'), accusing al-Ghazali, among many other things, of misunderstanding the whole question of the attributes of God. Averroës' impact on Islamic thought, however, was slight when compared to the enormous influence that he exerted in medieval Europe, which was rocked by a wave of 'Averroism' in the thirteenth century.

By the end of the thirteenth century the great vigour of Islamic philosophy was more or less spent. Commentaries gave birth to supercommentaries and glosses and little great and original work was produced between 1300 and 1800. The invasion of Egypt by Napoleon in 1798 produced an enormous culture shock in the Muslim world. The ensuing problem of how – or even, whether – to try to reconcile Western thought and culture with Islamic thought and traditional sciences is one that has still not been solved satisfactorily. Muslim thinkers like al-Afghani (1838–1897) and Muhammad Abduh (1849–1905) wrestled with this problem but, though imbued with Western ideas, they were at heart distrustful of the West and its culture. The most serious interpretation of Islam in modern philosophical terms in the twentieth century is that of Muhammad Iqbal (d. 1938). For Iqbal, Islam is not in opposition to philosophy but rather is the core of that total experience upon which philosophy must reflect; this is borne out by the Qur'an's emphasis on knowledge and reflection. Iqbal is critical, however, of the excessive reliance on reason exhibited by Ibn Rushd and the Mu'tazilah, on the one hand, and the anti-rationalism or scepticism of al-Ghazali, on the other (Fakhry, 1998:122). Western philosophies have also gained more Westernised adherents in the contemporary Islamic world who have written on Marxism, existentialism, logical positivism, and so on. 'But these Western oriented thinkers can hardly be characterized as Islamic; modern Muslim philosophers have yet to produce a system of philosophy that may be described as both truly Islamic and truly modern' (Flew, 1979:181–2).

Art and Architecture

'God is beautiful and likes beauty,' (Ibn Hanbal) said the Prophet Muhammad, as we read in the *Sahih* of Muslim and the *Musned* of Ibn Hanbal. He also said that, 'whenever one does something, God likes that one does it in a perfect manner' (Muslim). In the Qur'an, God says: 'Verily We have beautified the world's heaven with lamps' (67:5). The emphasis on beauty goes so far as to ordain in the Qur'an: 'O Children of Adam! Wear your beautiful adornment at every (*time and*) place of worship' (7:31).

The Qur'an took the initiative in the development of arts among Muslims. Its liturgical recitation created a new branch of music. The conservation of its text necessitated calligraphy. The construction of mosques developed architecture and decorative arts. To these were added later the secular needs of the society. The Qur'an itself (24:36) recommended grandeur in the construction of mosques. The Prophet's Mosque at Medina, the Dome of the Rock at Jerusalem, the Suleymaniye Mosque in Istanbul, the Taj Mahal at Agra, India, the Alhambra Palace at Granada and many other monuments are just some of the masterpieces of Islamic civilisation in architecture and artistic decoration.

Calligraphy, in particular, is a Muslim art and it is considered the ultimate achievement in Islamic arts. It makes writing a piece of art, in place of pictures; it is employed in painting or mural sculpture, and used to decorate fine cloth and other materials. Music and song have had their development among Muslims. As for poetry, the Prophet recognises: 'There are verses of poems which are full of wisdom, and there are discourses of orators which produce a magical effect.' The poetical works of Muslims are found in all languages and relate to all times. In short, Muslims have made a worthy contribution to the realm of art and architecture.

Two important characteristics may be mentioned concerning the function of the arts in traditional Islamic culture. First, they served to crystallise the abstract concepts of Islam into concrete form. Second, they integrated these concepts into the daily life of the people. Many of the arts attempt to convey the difficult-to-grasp concept of God's transcendence beyond the material world. In the visual arts this concept is emphasised by an avoidance of representational forms. In music the non-material quality of sound itself points to the spiritual experience of man and that experience is extolled also in the mystical poetry and prose of the Sufis. Didactic prose, on the other hand, sought to establish morals for everyday life. Calligraphy rendered visible the spoken word of God (Martin, 1996:158).

2

Theological Dimension:
Faith and Its Articles

According to Islamic theology, faith (*iman*) is simply defined *tasdiq*. *Tasdiq* is to recognise a truth, to appropriate it, to affirm it, to confirm it and to actualise it. Faith in its typically Islamic form has a distinctively close relationship with knowledge. This does not mean, however, that faith is considered as just knowledge. Faith is not merely knowledge; it includes knowledge, but is something else as well. That additional something is *tasdiq*. Faith is *tasdiq* based on knowledge, not on 'the leap of faith'. Thus, faith means not simply 'to believe' a proposition, but rather to recognise a truth and to existentialise it. In other words, faith may actually be caused by knowledge, but knowledge is far from constituting the essence of faith; faith is rather an 'assent' which is of such a nature that the person who has it feels a profound contentment arising from such an unshakeable conviction.

The most important of all the duties of a human being is the duty of reflection and reasoning for obtaining knowledge of God. The first thing to do is to reflect on created things, heaven and earth, human beings and living beings, and to infer from them the existence of the One who has created them. But exercising reflection and reasoning do not necessarily require passing through a process of reasoning in which logical syllogisms must be employed in their technical forms. The person is just expected to reflect upon the creations, the signs of God in the world, and infer from them, by exercising his or her reason, the existence of God.

The articles of faith in Islam are usually stated as six items. Muslims believe, first, in One God (*Allah*); second, in the angels created by Him; third, in the Holy Books given to the prophets; fourth, in the prophets through whom His revelations were brought to humankind; fifth, in the Day of Judgement in life after death; and sixth, in predestination. However, there are three basic ones, namely:

(a) belief in the Unity of God;

(b) belief in the prophethood of Muhammad; and

(c) belief in life after death and in man's accountability before God on the Day of Judgement.

Whoever professes these beliefs is a Muslim. We will now look at them in greater detail.

GOD (*ALLAH*)

Belief in God is the first and main article of Islamic faith. The Arabic word for one God is *Allah*, Lord and Creator of the universe. A Muslim should have an unshakeable belief in the existence and oneness of God. The universe itself and everything in the world proves that God exists. Belief in God and His great power alone can provide humanity with the best possible explanation of many mysterious things in the world and in life. He is the Creator of everything on earth and in the heavens. He is the Ruler and the Sustainer of the universe and there is no one else to share the creativity with Him.

As an uncompromising and pure monotheistic religion, according to Islam, God is one and unique (*tawhid*); and He has no partner, no children and no parents. He is eternal and everywhere. He is Creator of the universe, which is not self-explanatory. He is merciful, compassionate and loving. He sent prophets to guide humankind, to tell us how to live like good individuals and be happy in this world and the hereafter.

The God of Islam is both knowable and unknowable. Knowledge of God can be arrived at through different sources. The first and main source is revelation, the Qur'an. The other sources are the genuine sayings of the Prophet, our human ability of reasoning and observation and also internal experience. All of these sources and stages, however, will give us knowledge of God only in so far as He is related to us. But in His essential being and essence, we do not claim to have any knowledge of God. For it is said in the Qur'an (20:110) that, 'He knows (*all*) that is before them and (*all*) that is behind them, but they themselves cannot comprehend it with their knowledge.' Nevertheless, the Qur'an gives the most reliable and sufficient knowledge about God.

The first chapter of the Qur'an contains verses that succinctly describe some attributes of God and some aspects of the relationship between God and humankind:

> Praise be to Allah, the Lord of the Worlds; The Compassionate, the Merciful; Master of the Day of Judgement; You alone do we worship, and to You alone we pray for help; Guide us to the Straight Path; The way of those whom You have favoured; not of those who have incurred Your wrath. Nor of those who go astray. (1:2–7)

According to another verse from the middle of the Qur'an, which is more often quoted by the Sufis, 'Allah is the Light of the heavens and of the earth' (24:35). However, He is not only light but also love, as the following verses imply: 'He it is who originates and brings back to life. He is the Forgiving, the Loving' (85:13–14). The Qur'an states that God is love, but it does not identify God solely with love, for He is also knowledge, justice and majesty, as well as peace and beauty. But He is never without love and His love is essential to the creation of the universe and our relation with Him: 'Allah will bring a people whom He loves and who love Him' (5:54). In relation to God's nearness to human beings, it is also pointed out that 'We created man, and We know the promptings of his soul, and We are nearer to him than his jugular vein' (Qur'an 50:16).

The attributes of God are many and can be discovered in His names, but they can be summarised for the purpose of study under a few essential headings: life, eternity, unity, power, truth, beauty, justice, love and goodness. God is, thus, a living, self-subsisting, eternal and absolutely free creative reality which is one, all-powerful, all-knowing, all-beautiful, most just, most loving and all good. This description is neither too anthropomorphic nor too agnostic; it gives a limited but also a sufficient idea about the Islamic concept of God.

The doctrine of God the One, the Infinitely Good and All-Merciful, as stated in the Qur'an, not only emphasises utter transcendence, although there are powerful expressions of this truth. The Qur'an also accentuates God's nearness to us and that He is present everywhere: 'To Allah belongs the East and the West. Whichever way you turn, there is the face of Allah. Allah is All-Embracing, and All-Knowing' (2:115). So, the traditional religious life of a Muslim is based on a rhythmic movement between the poles of transcendence and immanence, of rigour and compassion, of justice and forgiveness, of the fear of punishment and hope for mercy based on God's love for us.

There may be hundreds of ways for seekers after truth to decide for themselves whether God exists or not. Some ways may be relatively personal, while others are more objective and have been discussed by many people more or less in the same structural form throughout the history of philosophy and theology. In Islamic thought, there are three traditional or classical arguments. The *kalam* cosmological argument based on the temporality (*huduth*) of the universe, the *falsafa* cosmological argument based on the contingency (*imkan*) of the universe, and the Qur'anic arguments from design. The latter were divided into two versions by Ibn Rushd, namely the argument from providence (*'inayah*) and the argument from creation (*ikhtira*). Muslim mystics, often referred to as Sufis, prefer to trust their direct or inner religious experience rather than rational arguments as the basic evidential ground of their belief.

Each individual may find a different form of argument convincing for his or her belief. Some arguments may simply appeal to religious experience and contemplation, while others are more scientific and philosophical. Some people may take up one argument by itself independently of the alternatives; others prefer to consider all the arguments and to take into account all the counter-arguments, and then make their final decision.

In Islamic thought, belief in the existence of God is considered to be innate in human nature, but only to such a degree that does not violate a person's freedom of belief or disbelief. We may develop this innate belief in three mutually supporting ways: through attending to revelation, through religious experience and through rational thought. We have already mentioned revelatory knowledge about God. Genuine religious experience is also worth taking seriously as a substantial ground for belief in God, either by the person who has the experience or by the person who is told of the experience, provided of course that the implications of the experience are in accord with the essence of our more objectively based background knowledge. The authoritative and strong religious experience of the great religious figures can best be explained as they commonly explain it themselves, that is, as the experience of the real presence, providence and guidance of God, and not at all as the result of a pathological personality. We will deal with the matter of religious and mystical experience in detail later.

Some Muslim scholars wrote independent books exclusively dealing with the teleological argument as proof of God's existence and attributes. One of them is attributed to al-Ghazali and is entitled *The Wisdom in God's Creatures* (1987). In this book, al-Ghazali explores wisdom in the creation of the heavens, the earth and living beings. In his analogical interpretation, the world is like a house and humans are like the owner of the house (1987:84). Everything in the world has been created in its best form and in conformity with human needs. All this wisdom in creatures is evidence for the exist- ence of an all-knowing, all-powerful God, who created them with a unique wisdom, who is free from all sorts of imperfection, and who has all the attributes of perfection (ibid.:85). In his *ar-Risalah al-Qudsiyyah* or in his *Ihya 'Ulum-al-Din*, al-Ghazali begins to explore the topic of the knowledge of God's existence by quoting this and other passages from the Qur'an:

> In the creation of the heavens and the earth; in the alternation of night and day; in the sailing of the ships through the ocean for the benefit of mankind; in the water which Allah sends down from the sky and with which He revises the earth after its death, and dispersing over it all kinds of beasts; in the ordinance of the winds and clouds that are driven between earth and sky: are signs for people who have sense. (2:164)

After quoting several such passages, al-Ghazali declares that it should be apparent to anyone with the minimum of intelligence, if he reflects a little upon the implication of these verses, and if he looks at the wonders in God's creation on earth and in the skies and at the wonders in animals and plants, that this marvellous, well-ordered system cannot exist without a maker who conducts it, and a creator who plans and perfects it (1965:33; cf. 1982:126). Al-Ghazali's reasoning here may be put in the simple form of a teleological argument, as follows

1. The world displays a well-ordered (or fine-tuned) system.

2. This marvellous system cannot (be expected to) exist without a maker and creator.

3. Therefore, there must be a maker and creator of this system.

Ibn Rushd also showed a definite predilection for the two versions of the teleological argument, which, according to him, had a basis in the Qur'an and were more compelling than other arguments. In his interpretation, two arguments for the existence of God are recommended in the Qur'an. The first is the argument from providence (*'inayah*) which runs as follows: everything in the world is adapted to humankind's existence and needs and reveals providence. For example, day and night, sun and moon, the four seasons, the earth and everything therein, animals and vegetables, rain, rivers, seas and so on, and also the well-adapted organs of the human and animal body, are all obviously suitable and adapted for human existence and needs. The adaptation and functionality exhibited throughout the world requires an agent who intends and wills it, for it cannot conceivably be due to chance (Ibn Rushd 1968:65, 66). What Ibn Rushd argues here is not that the whole universe has been created just for the sake of humankind. He disagrees with such an idea in his *Tahafut al-Tahafut* (1969:295). He defends, however, the argument that the universe is suitable for the existence and needs of humankind. This argument can simply be schematised as follows:

1. Everything in the world is suitable for the existence and needs of human beings.

2. This suitability cannot be achieved by chance.

3. Therefore, it is by necessity due to an agent intending to do so.

Rumi defends the same idea of a purposeful universe in relation to God and humankind in a poetic form with support of some analogies:

Does any painter paint a beautiful picture for the sake of the picture itself?

Nay, his object is to please children or recall departed friends to the memory of those who loved them.

Does any potter mould a jug for the jug's sake and not in hope of water?

Does any calligrapher write for the writing's sake and not for the benefit of the reader?

[...]

When the barriers in front and behind are lifted, the eye penetrates and reads the tablet of the Invisible.

Such a clairvoyant looks back to the origin of existence – he sees the

angels dispute with the Almighty as to making our Father (Adam)
His vicegerent. (Rumi, 1950:112)

Ibn Rushd's second proof, called the argument from creation, takes into
consideration animals, plants and the heavens. It is based on two principles:
that all beings are created and that everything created is in need of a creator.
The examples given refer, in particular, to life but also to perception and consciousness in animate beings. Heavenly bodies are thought to serve living
bodies on earth with their regular and stable motions. When we see that
bodies devoid of life are endowed with life, we know by necessity that there
is an inventor and creator of life, namely God (1968:65, 66). Ibn Rushd's
argument from creation can be stated in simple terms as follows:

1. Bodies devoid of life are created as living beings; in other words,
    they are endowed with life (and, in some cases, with perception
    and consciousness).

2. The real cause of this creation (of life, perception and consciousness)
    can be neither earthly nor heavenly bodies, which are in the service
    of life but devoid of it.

3. Therefore, there must be an agent who created life (perception and
    consciousness).

It may seem paradoxical, but this classical argument is in fact very
modern as well. It stands up to Hume's major objections to the teleological
argument and to the objections raised by the theory of evolution. Its main
emphasis is on the origin of life. Moreover, from the beginning, it is ready
to accept some causal contribution of inanimate beings, such as heavenly
bodies, to the origination and continuation of living beings, but insists that
the real cause and the true basis for the explanation of life and consciousness
requires the existence of a creator God.

After the teleological arguments we should examine the *kalam* cosmological argument in Islamic theology. This is an argument advanced and
most commonly used by Muslim theologians, or *kalam* scholars. It starts
with the idea of the temporality of the universe and through the principle of
causality and the impossibility of actual infinite regress of temporal causes,
arrives at the existence of a determinant and creator God. Its crucial premise,
which asserts a temporal beginning for the universe using traditional philosophical arguments, has received strong empirical support from scientific
developments in recent years. The Big Bang theory and the second law of
thermodynamics strongly suggest that the universe did have a beginning.
Consequently, this argument represents a much sounder argument for establishing belief in God in the present situation of scientific cosmology than
in medieval times. Since everything that begins to exist has a cause for its
existence and since the universe began to exist in the Big Bang, then the
universe logically has a personal cause and creator of its existence, who

freely chooses the time of creation and makes it possible through his great power and knowledge.

The *kalam* cosmological argument presupposes the temporality of the universe, and present scientific cosmology does seem to support it. But the *falsafa* cosmological argument is readily compatible with the idea of the universe having always existed. So it complements the *kalam* argument in one sense to arrive at a cumulative case argument, as the *kalam* argument complemented the teleological arguments and they complemented the argument from religious experience.

The *falsafa* cosmological argument was mainly developed by philosophers like al-Farabi and Ibn Sina and was always their preferred argument. According to it, the universe is the total of possible or contingent beings and, as such, it is not self-subsistent and therefore requires a necessarily existent being to sustain it. As a result, this approach, too, argues strongly in favour of the existence of God in terms of metaphysical certainty, even for someone who believes in the eternality of the universe. Since the universe exists and since that which begins to exist owes its existence to the action of a cause, which outweighs its non-existence and continually maintains it in existence, then, the universe logically terminates in a cause that holds its existence of itself, and this is the first cause, the self-existent being, namely, the one God, who has great power, knowledge and goodness, and who can easily be found in genuine religious experiences and in the magnificent beauty of nature (Yaran, 2003:200).

ANGELS

The second article of Islamic faith is to believe in the angels (*malak*) of God. Angels are spiritual beings. They have no material body, no physical desires and no material needs; nor do they have any masculinity or femininity. Allah has creatures in several shapes: some of them are perceptible to the human eye and some are not. We cannot deny their presence just because we do not see, smell, touch, taste or hear them; instead, we must acknowledge their existence. They are the beloved servants of Allah. God gave the angels separate functions and they do their duties according to His commands and do not disdain from His service. They have no share in God's divinity and no authority to do anything of their own accord. Their total number is only known by Allah. According to the Qur'an, the angel who brought revelation (*wahy*) to the Prophet is called Jibril (Jibrail, Gabriel). In Islamic belief Jibril, who is also described in the Qur'an as the 'trustworthy spirit' (*al-ruh al-amin*), stands above all the angels. In the sayings of the Prophet Muhammad, we read that this celestial messenger, Jibril, did not appear to the Prophet always in the same form. The Prophet sometimes saw him as a being suspended in the air, sometimes in the shape of a man, or sometimes as a being with wings.

The highest degree of contact and the most infallible means of communication between man and his creator is called *wahy* by the Prophet. This is not ordinary inspiration, but a veritable revelation made to man by the Lord. God is omnipresent and, as the Qur'an says, He is 'nearer to man than his jugular vein' (50:16); yet no physical contact is possible with Him. Therefore, it is an angel who serves as intermediary or the channel through which God's message is transmitted to His human agent or messenger, namely, the Prophet. These divine messages or revelations constitute the holy books.

HOLY BOOKS

Therefore, the third Islamic article of faith is to believe in the Holy Books of God. For Muslims, God gave guidance to humankind through the prophets in the form of scrolls or books. The Qur'an names the scrolls of Abraham, the Torah of Moses, the Psalter of David and the Gospel of Jesus as the books revealed by God to the prophets before the Prophet Muhammad. Nevertheless, for Muslims the sacred book is the Qur'an. A Muslim believes in all the earlier books of God in general, but follows the Qur'an alone. The Qur'an today is exactly as it was revealed to the Prophet Muhammad. In the early years of his mission, the Prophet Muhammad used to repeat aloud, during the course of revelation, what was revealed to him. Soon, however, he abandoned this habit of simultaneous repeating and began to remain silent till the end of the state of revelation and then he communicated the message of God to his secretaries who recorded it. This process is described in the Qur'an (75:16, 17): 'Do not move your tongue (*with the revelation*) so that you may hasten (*committing*) it (*to memory*). It is for Us to collect it and to promulgate it.'

A Muslim believes in the Qur'an, reads some parts of it daily and tries to follow it in his or her life. The Qur'an deals with all the subjects which concern us as human beings: theological doctrine, worship, morality and wisdom, but its basic theme is the relationship between God and His creatures. At the same time it provides guidelines for a virtuous and peaceful society.

The necessity for revelation is attested by the facts of life; the very condition of finitude, in which we find ourselves, calls for divine help. In the short span of life that is given to us, it would be impossible for us, because of the limited range of our capabilities and powers of perception, to understand our role here below and to plan wise and intelligent action with a view to servicing the essential needs of our being without divine assistance. Reflection shows that even the best trained philosophers have found it difficult to develop cogent answers, in spite of having dedicated the bulk of their time to solving the great intellectual questions concerning the explanation of being and the meaning of life. Hence, the holy books provide answers to these questions on the authority of the prophets who received their revelation from God.

PROPHETS

The fourth article of faith in Islam is to believe in the prophets, as is stated in the Qur'an: 'The Messenger believes in what has been revealed to him by his Lord, and so do the believers. They all believe in Allah and His angels, His scriptures and His messengers' (2:285). For Muslims, God gave His guidance through the prophets and sent prophets to all people at different times. It is said in the Qur'an that 'for every people a guide has been provided' (13:7). In Qur'anic terminology, the human agent of the divine message is called variously *nabi* (prophet), *rasul* (messenger), *mursal* (envoy), *bashir* (announcer), *nadhir* (warner), and so on. They were men of great virtue and character, the true spiritual leaders and guides of human society. Nevertheless, a prophet is a human being like us, with the difference that he receives guidance or revelation from God. A Muslim believes in, loves and respects all the prophets whose names are mentioned in the Qur'an. Muslims believe in the existence of a large number of prophets (traditionally given as 124,000) sent to all people. This large number of prophets indicates implicitly that all nations must have been given divine guidance through the prophets or messengers sent to them by God. Although generally only applied to the Abrahamic tradition, the principle of the universality of revelation encompasses all nations.

It was through the grace of Allah and His mercy to humankind that He sent messengers. They showed the true principles of faith, the genuine way of worship and the true ethics. They were mediators between God and His creatures. Prophethood is the gift of God. He bestows it upon whom He wishes and it cannot be obtained through strife. An angel brings the message of God to a chosen man and the latter is charged with its communication to the people. Prophets are men of great piety and models of good behaviour.

According to the Qur'an, there were certain prophets who received the revelation of divine books and there were others who did not receive new books but had to follow the books revealed to their predecessors. The divine messages do not disagree on fundamental truths, such as the Oneness of God, the obligation to do good and abstain from evil, and so on, yet they may differ as to the rules of social conduct depending on the social evolution of a particular people.

For Muslims, Muhammad is the Last Prophet and Messenger. The mission of the Prophet Muhammad is not to invent a new religion, but to return the monotheistic religion of Abraham back to its original purity and to present it in its excellent form. In the Qur'an, the Prophet Muhammad is given the following instructions: 'Say: "I am not an innovation among the messengers, nor do I know what will be done with me or with you. I follow but that which is revealed to me by inspiration; I am but a warner open and clear"' (46:9). For Muslims, he who follows Muhammad follows all the prophets. For whatever was good and eternally workable in their teachings has been embodied in his teaching. Indeed, he is singled out in the Qur'an as 'the messenger of Allah and the Seal of the Prophets' (33:40), the one whose imprint on history is as final as a wax seal on a letter.

LIFE AFTER DEATH

The fifth article of Islamic faith is belief in life after death. The life of this world and all that is in it will come to an end on a divinely appointed date, which is called the Last Day (*Qıyamat*). All human beings who have lived in the world will then be restored to life and will be presented before God. This is called resurrection (*Hashr*). The entire record of every person will be presented before God for final judgement (*Hisab*). Those who excel in goodness will be rewarded. Those whose evils and wrongdoings outweigh their good deeds will be punished. Those who are condemned and deserve punishment will be sent to hell (*Jahannam*). Those who emerge successfully from the final judgement will go to paradise (*Cannat*).

Belief in a life after death is one of the most fundamental and central religious tenets together with belief in the existence of God. Of all the world religions, Islam is the one which has most strongly and centrally taught the reality and importance of an eternal life beyond this temporary life on earth. It regards it as one of the most essential articles of faith. The Qur'an mentions belief in life after death together with belief in the existence of God: 'Those who believe (in the Qur'an), those who follow the Jewish (scriptures), and the Sabians and the Christians, – Any who believe in Allah, and the Last Day, and work righteousness, – on them shall be no fear, nor shall they grieve' (5:69). The term 'hereafter' (*al-'akhira*) is used in the Qur'an more than one hundred times; and there is even a chapter (Surah 75) called 'The Resurrection'.

The concepts of life after death found in the various religious and philosophical traditions of the world can be divided into two broad categories: non-actual and non-personal life after death (such as immortality by remembrance in this world or by union with the One), and actual and personal life after death. Needless to say, Islamic religion and thought have held the latter view. According to the Qur'an, life in the hereafter is incomparably more real and actual than life in this world: 'This life of the present is nothing but (temporary) enjoyment: It is the Hereafter that is the Home that will last' (40:39). Life after death will also be a personal one, and individual resurrection, accountability and destiny will occur in the hereafter. Each human being is responsible for his or her belief and behaviour at the Day of Judgement and no man can save another. The Qur'an states that: 'O Mankind! do your duty to your Lord and fear (the coming of) a Day when no father can avail aught for his son, nor a son avail aught for his father' (31:33).

The second category above, actual and personal life after death, can be divided into two subcategories: actual and personal life after death in this world, and actual and personal life after death in another sphere of existence which is different from this one. Mainstream Islamic thought does not accept the former view. The Qur'an rejects the unrighteous man's demand for another chance of life in this world in Surah 23:99,100: 'Until, when death comes to one of them, he says: 'O my Lord! send me back (to life), in order that I may work righteousness in the things I neglected.' – 'By no means! It is but a word he says.' Before them is a Partition till the Day they are raised up.'

Therefore, it is this second subcategory, the nature of actual and personal life after death in the hereafter, that deserves real concern from the mainstream Islamic point of view. The proclamation of the resurrection, the Day of Judgement and the eternal destiny granted with it comes at the beginning of the Qur'anic teachings. The Qur'an describes the resurrection in these terms: 'One day the Earth will be changed to a different Earth, and so will be the Heavens, and (men) will be marshalled forth, before Allah, the One, the Irresistible' (14:48). On the Day of Judgement all the race of Adam will be gathered together, each one to receive judgement and everlasting retribution according to his or her beliefs and deeds in this world: 'The balance that day will be true (to a nicety): Those whose scale (of good) will be heavy, will prosper: Those whose scale will be light, will find their souls in perdition, for that day wrongfully treated Our Signs' (7:8–9).

When the idolaters of Mecca denied the reality and even the possibility, of life after death, the Qur'an exposed the weakness of their stand and of those who had thought like them by advancing rational arguments in support of it: 'He says, "Who can give life to (dry) bones and decomposed ones (at that)?" Say, "He will give them life Who created them for the first time.... Is not He Who created the heavens and the earth able to create the like thereof?"' (36:78–81)

This is the basic Qur'anic and thus undisputedly Islamic understanding of life after death and an important argument for it. Within the circle of these basic beliefs and concepts there have been some differences of opinion and interpretation in the history of Islamic thought. There are two different views about what happens at the moment of death and during the period between death and resurrection. Does the soul die or disappear at physical death and is it brought back to life on the last day, or does death belong only to the body while the human soul continues to exist after its separation from the body? According to some scholars, Ibn Qayyım al-Jawzıyyah says, the soul dies and has a taste of death because 'Every soul shall have a taste of death' (Qur'an, 21:35). For others, including himself, souls do not die because they were created for eternity; death belongs only to bodies. For this group of scholars both the verses of the Qur'an and the sayings of the Prophet indicate that after death the human soul can do without the body until the resurrection of the body. Allah says in the Qur'an (3:169): 'Think not of those who are slain in Allah's way as dead. Nay, they live, finding their sustenance from their Lord.' The view of the first group of scholars could be called 're-creation', and the view of the second group of scholars, which is tradition-ally more common among both the scholars and the people, could be called 'resurrection'.

According to one traditional interpretation, *resurrection* means that the body is resurrected to be rejoined with a continuing soul. The bodies mentioned here are not meant to be the same bodies as in this world. Rather, it is an appropriate body for the different spiritual structure of the world to come.

Many medieval and contemporary Muslim philosophers and scholars believe in resurrection and defend it. Avicenna (Ibn Sina) says in his book *al-Najat* that 'the soul does not die with the death of the body and is abso-lutely incorruptible'. According to al-Ghazali, death is only a change of state and the soul survives after its separation from the body, remaining either in a miserable or in a happy condition until the day of resurrection. For Fakhr al-Din al-Razi, another important figure in the history of Islamic philosophico-theological thought, the human being is alive when the body is dead, or in other words, the human being lives after death. He brings some of the verses of the Qur'an and some sayings of the Prophet as evidence for the truth of this view. One such is the case of the people of Pharaoh, mentioned in the Qur'an: 'The Fire of Hell: they are exposed to it morning and evening; and on the day when the Hour of Resurrection comes, (*a voice will cry*) 'Let the people of Pharaoh enter the more awful punishment!'' (40:46). In his view, this verse and some sayings of the Prophet show that life between death and the day of resurrection is not peculiar to martyrs or believers but includes every human being. Contemporary traditionalist writers are in agreement with their predecessors that in some senses the dead are aware of the living; they do not die with death of their body and continue to exist (Smith and Haddad, 1981:104).

There is a special concept used in Islamic understanding of death and resurrection: *barzakh*. *Barzakh* is a state, perhaps some kind of suspense between death and resurrection. After departing from the physical body, the soul does not enter its life in heaven or hell at once. It remains suspended in the ethereal world. Here its faculties remain in abeyance, though intact, and this state will continue until the hour of resurrection. In many instances the life of the *barzakh* is seen as a particular stage in the development of human life. The three levels of physical development – dust, embryo and birth – are compared to the three stages of spiritual development. The first is this life, the third is the resurrection, and the second is the stage that intervenes between these two, called *barzakh*.

For some Muslim scholars or writers, however, death and immortality in Islam must be understood not as a resurrection, as defined and described above, but as a re-creation. *Re-creation* means that individual persons are re-created sometime after their death. There is no literal immortality, no persisting soul, but simply life after death. Human existence is gap-inclusive: we live, die and our bodies disintegrate, and in the future we are re-created to live again. What is re-created is our entire psychophysical being, which, although it allows the re-created to be the same person as the deceased, might have many features (for example, appearance, physical composition, lack of certain diseases) that differ from those we have now. As al-Ghazali states, some people thought that death was a state of non-entity until the day of resurrection and that there was neither reward nor punishment in the grave in this period. For him, this opinion is corrupt (*Ihya*: 451). Those who advocate re-creation see the human being not as an eternal soul temporarily attached to a mortal body, but as a form of finite, mortal, psychophysical life. In their understanding, death means sheer unqualified extinction – passing out from the lighted circle of life into 'death's dateless night'. Only through the sovereign creative love of God can there be a new existence beyond the grave. Thus, life after death is not inherently present in human nature which, as it were, follows its own course of fruition, but is exclusively dependent on God's will and omnipotence. God, however, has promised to re-create human beings after death and will give them a form of existence fully commensurate with their bodily acts, psychological states and spiritual achievements.

Those who defend the view of resurrection as a concept of life after death have appealed to *a posteriori* arguments for the existence of the soul and its survival of bodily death, as well as to *a priori* arguments. *A posteriori* arguments based, particularly, on paranormal experiences and spiritualist writings have been regarded as strong empirical proof for traditional religious ideas and against materialistic views concerning human nature and destiny. Those who defend the re-creationist concept of life after death, however, have to appeal exclusively to *a priori* arguments based either on religious and scriptural authorities or on ethical considerations. For, unlike the doctrine of the soul, life after death is not guaranteed by any continuing thing. If there is to be life after death, it requires the intervention of an omnipotent and omniscient God. Moreover, God's omnibenevolence seems as important as God's omnipotence and omniscience. In Muwahidi's view, for example, the evidence or guarantee of life after death is God's will, omnipotence and promise in the Qur'an. Although not essentially immortal, he says, the individual will be re-created by God after death. So, practically speaking, death does not finally extinguish the person. God has promised to give human beings everlasting life and He does not fail in His promise (Muwahidi, 1989:43). He brings evidence from the Qur'an: 'Every soul shall have a taste of death. And only on the Day of Judgement shall you be paid your full recompense' (3:185).

For some writers, the Qur'an not only informs people about the hereafter but also gives answers and arguments about life after death which are based on the rational principles drawn from observations of nature and a knowledge of the events that occur every time. One of these simple rational principles is as follows: making a difficult thing includes making an easier one. Someone who made something can make its similar and can make it again. God created human beings for the first time. Therefore, it is possible for God to re-create individuals after death; because it is easier. The central notion in this reasoning is God's omnipotence. Other considerations focus on God's moral attributes.

One of the ethical arguments for life after death relies on divine justice. Not everything seems to be just in this world and not everybody finds the equivalent of what he or she deserves. But since there is a God who is just, then there must be a world where justice will be manifested absolutely. In addition, it seems that God's wisdom is also referred to in this evidential context. For instance, Iqbal affirms that, 'It is highly improbable that a being whose evolution has taken millions of years should be thrown away as a thing of no use' (1986:119).

The vast majority of Muslims continue to uphold the various versions of the traditional idea of bodily resurrection, supporting their views with the evidence of modern parapsychology, in addition to the foundational *a priori* religious and ethical arguments. On the other hand, the idea of bodily re-creation after a period of nonentity has also found advocates both among some scholars, who claim that the Qur'anic understanding of human nature is actually a monistic one, and philosophers or philosophically minded writers, who are well informed about modern criticisms of Cartesian dualism. But both those who believe in the concept of resurrection and those who believe in re-creation agree on some basic principles of faith: for both, the hope of future life depends on the existence and action of God rather than on the immortality of the soul or its own natural power. Moreover, both of them also agree with the general idea that there will be a day of resurrection and human accountability, followed by eternal life for all human beings.

According to the Qur'an, 'Allah has promised the believers, men and women, gardens beneath which rivers flow, to dwell therein, and beautiful mansions in Gardens of Paradise. But the good pleasure of Allah is greater still. That is the supreme triumph' (9:72). So, for those who are capable of understanding and appreciating the abstract notion of the other world, the opportunity to contemplate God would be the greatest and real reward of the Believer. It is in the light of this authoritative interpretation that one should read what the Qur'an and the *hadith* unceasingly describe for the common man as the joys of paradise and the horrors of hell, in terms which remind us of our surroundings in this world. It is necessary to speak to everyone according to his or her capacity of understanding and intelligence. All this is easily explained when one thinks of the vast majority of people, of the masses, to whom the divine message is addressed and who are the intended recipients of eternal salvation. In our present state, we can scarcely imagine the real bliss that will come to us in the hereafter. Indeed, the Qur'an says that, 'No soul knows what is kept hid for them of joy (*delights of the eyes*), as a reward for what they used to do' (32:17). But it is also emphasised that it will be more than the greatest good: 'For those who do good is the greatest good, and even more. Neither darkness nor shame shall cover their faces. They are the owners of the Garden, dwelling there forever' (10:26).

FATE AND FREE WILL

Belief in fate, together with human free will, is often considered as the sixth article of Islamic faith. This belief, however, does not in any way make a Muslim either fatalist or determinist. It simply draws the demarcation line between what is God's knowledge and power and what is man's freedom and responsibility. God's eternal knowledge and power do not prevent us from making our own plans within our own limited sphere of freedom of choice and power of actualisation. For God has given man the right of selection and self-determination. He is free to do as he wishes; and therefore he is responsible for his actions. According to the Qur'an, this is the truth revealed by God to His successive messengers, from Abraham to Muhammad: 'Or has he not had news of what is in the books of Moses, and Abraham who fulfilled his duty: That no soul shall bear another's burden. And that each can have nothing save what he strives for, and that his effort will be seen. And afterward he will be repaid for it with fullest payment' (53:36–41).

The eternal dilemma of divine predestination and human free will cannot easily be resolved by logic alone. For, if man enjoys free will in all his actions, the omnipotence and omniscience of God seems to suffer. Similarly, if God predestines, why should man be held responsible for his acts? The Prophet Muhammad emphatically recommended his adherents not to engage in discussions on this topic, 'which has led astray those people who preceded you' (as Ibn Hanbal, Tirmidhi and others report). So, Muslims believe both in God's fate and in human free will.

According to Islam, the human nature is neither completely good nor completely bad; by contrast, man is a two-dimensional creature from an ethical and psychological perspective, with an innate disposition towards virtue, knowledge and beauty; this disposition may guide a person towards the right way but not to the extent of violating that individual's freedom. The human species is capable of choosing freely both good and evil, right and wrong. This phenomenon is expressed in the following verses from the Qur'an: 'By the Soul and Him that formed it, then inspired it with (*knowledge of*) sin and piety: He has indeed prospered who purifies it, and he who stunts it is ruined' (91:7–8). This means that every person has the natural faculty of distinguishing between right and wrong, good and bad, piety and sin. Each of us can make a choice, which may be right or wrong, and can act freely in accordance with that choice.

Human nature is one of the main reasons for most of the moral evil and suffering in the world; for while some of us prefer to choose the right way in the special circumstances of free choice, others may choose wrongly, misusing their God-given or innate freedom of choice and action. Some may object to this view and may question why a good God did not create us so that we would always choose the right way. This question is not too difficult to answer. Being open to evil as well as to good does seem to be a necessary condition of being a free agent; and freedom is worth having for human beings even in the face of occasional misuse. For what makes an action and its agent really valuable is the condition that it was chosen and accomplished freely, not through any external compulsion.

However, how can a human being use his free will in the right direction, and how can he purify his ego from selfish corruption and become a perfect human being in his intentions, emotions, thoughts and behaviour? According to Islam, the first requirement is to have faith, as described above, and the second is to do good works and to worship. This second, more practical part is generally codified as the 'Five Pillars' of Islam.

3

Practical Dimension:
The Five Pillars of Islam

There are five pillars on which the whole structure of Islam stands. While God, the Qur'an and the Prophet Muhammad unite all Muslims in their common belief, the Five Pillars of Islam provide a unity of practice among them. Islamic practices simultaneously affect the body and the soul. Not only do temporal practices acquire a sacred moral character, when they conform to divine prescriptions, but spiritual practices also possess a material utility. The pillars of Islam are the five essential obligatory practices that all Muslims are expected to perform: the profession of faith; prayer; almsgiving; fasting; and pilgrimage to Mecca.

PROFESSION OF FAITH

The first pillar is the profession of faith (*shahadah*), namely the declaration that 'There is no God but Allah and Muhammad is Allah's Messenger.' This brief testimony marks a person's entry into the Islamic faith and community. It affirms Islam's absolute monotheism and acceptance of Muhammad as God's last messenger. The words have to be uttered, with sincere conviction and under no coercion.

This faith is followed by action, namely by the other four pillars in relation to worship, since it is believed that faith and action must go together. Faith in the heart must lead to good actions and morals in every aspect of life. In Islam, salvation lies in doing good deeds and not merely in faith. Nevertheless, if a Muslim fails to perform or practice some of the other pillars properly, then he or she is considered to have committed a sin, but does not cease to be a Muslim. Worship (*'ibadah*), according to Islam, is not only a means of purifying the soul but it also encompasses all practical aspects of life which must be in accordance with the law of God and for His pleasure.

PRAYER

The second pillar of Islam is prayer (*salat*) or the service of worship, which is considered to be the foundation of Islam. Muslims pray five times a day: they should pray when they rise – early in the morning, at dawn (*fajr*) – again at midday (*zuhr*), late in the afternoon (*asr*), after sunset (*maghrib*) and at night before they go to bed (*isha*). This applies to every adult, man or woman since responsibility for worship is acquired after puberty for all mature, sane adults. Although the prayers are compulsory and should be performed within specified periods, there is still sufficient flexibility to prevent real inconvenience. Prayers missed due to reasons beyond one's control can be made up later. Travellers are permitted by the Prophet to shorten their services of four *rak'ats*, celebrating only two *rak'ats*. According to some religious schools, in very special circumstances, and when travelling, the two afternoon and the two evening prayers can be performed together. For instance, the second and third, between midday and sunset, at any moment, and the fourth and the fifth any time during the night.

Ablution or ritual washing and physical cleanliness is a prerequisite for the validity of a service of worship. For this ritual purification, you have to wash the hands, the mouth, the nose, the face, the arms, the head, the ears and the feet. Washing is not merely a sign of outward cleanliness, it is repentance for the past and a resolution for the future. After sexual intercourse, it is necessary for both husband and wife to take a complete bath before they can pray. In all parts of the globe, the faithful turn their faces during the service of worship towards the same focal point (*Qiblah*), the Kaaba in Mecca. This reminds them of the unity of the world community of Muslims, without distinctions of class, race or region.

The early afternoon service is transformed every Friday into a weekly congregational service; this is performed with greater solemnity, usually in a mosque, and the *imam* of the locality also gives a sermon before prayer.

Islam has instituted two annual feasts: one at the end of the fasting month and the other on the occasion of the pilgrimage to Mecca. These two feasts are celebrated by two special services of prayer, in addition to the daily five. Another service of prayer, of restricted obligation, is held for the deceased before burial.

For Muslims, prayer is a direct link between the worshipper and God, and it helps the faithful to remember God and to follow His commands. Prayer is a regular and disciplined act of worship in which, mentally and physically, Muslims humbly submit themselves to God, to praise Him, to glorify Him, to repent to Him and to seek mercy, forgiveness and guidance from Him. It keeps individuals away from evil and reminds them that they are responsible for all of their actions. It also reinforces a sense of belonging to a single, worldwide community of believers.

ALMSGIVING

The third pillar is almsgiving, obligatory charity or welfare money for the poor (*zakat*). For most purposes, this involves the payment each year of two and a half per cent of one's capital or accumulated wealth and assets, excluding such items as primary residence, car and professional tools. Only certain people are qualified to receive obligatory charity. There are, of course, other forms of charity over and above the obligatory zakat, which can be donated to such recipients as seem appropriate.

Islam stands for brotherhood and social justice and it asserts that the poor and the needy have rights to the wealth of the rich. Payment of almsgiving represents the duty to care for the community's social welfare. It is a great sin not to share one's wealth with the needy and to let them suffer from hunger and disease. Zakat is a duty enjoined by God and undertaken by Muslims in the interest of society as a whole. However, it is also of human-itarian and socio-political value as well as being motivated by spiritual and moral concerns. It is an effective instrument for cultivating the spirit of social responsibility on the part of the contributor and the feeling of security and belonging on the part of the recipient. The Qur'an says 'Those who spend their wealth by night and day, in private and public shall be rewarded by their Lord. No fear shall come upon them, neither shall they grieve' (2:274).

FASTING

The fourth pillar is fasting (*sawm*) during the ninth month, *Ramadan*, of the Islamic calendar. For all healthy, adult Muslims, fasting begins at daybreak and ends at sunset; therefore, between dawn and sunset, they must abstain from eating, drinking and sexual relations.

Those who are sick, elderly, or on a journey and also women who are pregnant or nursing are permitted to break the fast and make up an equal number of days later in the year or pay the equivalent of one day's food for each day of fasting missed to help the poor. Children begin to fast from puberty.

It is a means of spiritual training, self-discipline and self-purification. God states in the Qur'an: 'O you who believe! Fasting is prescribed for you, as it was prescribed for those who came before you; that you will perhaps guard yourselves (*against evil*)' (2:183). The month of Ramadan is a special time for Muslims everywhere; a time for reflection and greater spirituality. It is a test of moral character, an education and an opportunity to mediate. If performed with the sincere intention of pleasing God, the fast is much more than a physical endurance test and becomes a most fulfilling and enrich-ing act of spiritual dedication. It should also lead to a special endeavour to abstain from all evil and sinful acts. The month of Ramadan ends with a great celebration, Eid ul-Fitr, the Feast of the Breaking of the Fast, one of the two great annual religious feasts and holy days.

PILGRIMAGE

The fifth pillar of Islam is the pilgrimage (*Hajj*). The pilgrimage involves visiting the Kaaba in Mecca at least once in one's lifetime, if one can afford it physically and financially. Those who do not posses the material means of travel are exempted. Each year over two million Muslims of all colours and from all countries, men or women, gather in Mecca in the twelfth month of the Islamic calendar and worship God. The Islamic year is lunar; consequently, Hajj occurs throughout all seasons during one's lifetime.

Pilgrims enter a state of sacredness where arguing and fighting, cutting a plant or even harming a fly is prohibited. They wear simple garments that strip away distinctions of class and culture. This strengthens the spirit of unity, equality and brotherhood. The believers, without distinctions of race, language, birthplace or even class, feel the obligation to go there and to mix with one another in a spirit of fraternal equality before God. The pilgrimage ends with the celebration of a great feast, Eid ul-Adha or the Feast of Sacrifice, and the sacrificial meat is distributed to the needy.

These characteristics of the five pillars of Islam show that spiritual duties are not devoid of material advantages and temporal duties also have their spiritual value. But all the benefits arising from them in this world and in the hereafter are dependent on good intentions and motives that are supported and improved by Islamic ethics and morality, as well as Islamic belief.

4

Ethical Dimension:
Moral Values and Virtues

In the general Islamic view, the correct performance of religious duties and the right understanding of religious doctrine are inseparable elements of the moral life. Within this comprehensive structure, however, certain forms of conduct are more particularly designated by the term *adab* and especially *akhlak*. The Prophet Muhammad even said that 'I have been sent to fulfil the virtues which go with nobility of character (*makarim al-akhlak*)'.

It would be too lengthy to cite here all the ethical exhortations (*akhlak*) of the Qur'an or Islam. The basic moral advice may be found in a surah from the Qur'an. First, there are at least seven positive commands: to know but one God; to be kind to parents; to be righteous; to give to the poor; to be moderate in spending; to be kind in speaking and to be generous:

> Your Lord has decreed that you worship none but Him, and that you show kindness to your parents. If either or both of them attain old age with you, (*show no sign of impatience, and*) do not (*even*) say 'fie' to them; nor rebuke them, but speak kind words to them. And lower unto them the wing of humility and tenderness and say: 'Lord, be merciful to them both, as they did care for me when I was small.' Your Lord best knows what is in your minds. If you are righteous, He surely was ever Forgiving to those who turn (*to Him*). Give to the near of kin their due, and also the destitute and the wayfarer, and do not squander your substance wastefully.... But if you turn away from them (*the needy*), because you are still waiting for your Lord's bounty that you are expecting, then (*at least*) speak to them a kind word. Do not tie your hand to your neck (*do not be miserely*) nor stretch it without any restraint (*do not be extravagant*) for then you should sit down rebuked, denuded (17:23–9).

Then, there are also seven definite prohibitions in the following verses. Muslims must desist from the practice of infanticide, from adultery, from killing unjustly, from robbing orphans, from cheating in trade, from believing false reports and from showing pride:

Do not slay your offspring for fear of want. It is We who provide for them, and for you. Indeed their killing is a great sin. Do not approach adultery, for it is an indecent thing and an evil way. Do not take the life which Allah has rendered sacrosanct, except for a just cause.... Do not approach the property of an orphan except in the way that is best (*responsible investment*) until he attains majority. Keep your covenants, for one is responsible for one's covenant. Give full measure when you measure, and weigh with even scales (*when you weigh*). This is better, and will be the best in the end. Do not go after that of which you have no knowledge, for (*man's*) eyes, ears and heart, each of these (*senses*) shall be closely questioned. Do not walk proudly on the earth (Qur'an, 17:31–7).

As regards daily relations with others, the Prophet Muhammad himself also declared the most essential formula of morality, sometimes referred to as the Islamic expression of the 'golden rule' in ethics: 'None of you is a believer if he does not like for his brother exactly that which he likes for his own self' (al-Bukhari).

In addition to individual values and virtues, the peace and security offered by a stable family unit and a virtuous society are greatly valued in Islam and seen as essential for the spiritual growth of its members. In Islamic morality, the origin and end of all actions is God's will and consent. Belief in the resurrection of the body and the Day of Judgement has added to moral behaviour an eschatological dimension of human responsibility and accountability.

The number of cardinal virtues is not strictly determined in Islamic ethics. Kindness and equity, compassion and mercy, generosity, self-restraint, sincerity, the moral fellowship of the believers, honesty, truthfulness, the keeping of commitments, fair-dealing, humility, patience, endurance, courage, thankfulness, dignity, purity, modesty and chastity, helpfulness, cooperation, charitableness, hospitality, brotherliness, warmth and lovingness, striving and hard work are among the virtues of Islamic morality. Nevertheless, a short and very well-known verse in the Qur'an commands three main virtues and forbids three main vices: 'Allah commands justice and kindness and charity to one's kindred, and forbids indecency, wickedness and oppression. He admonishes you so that you may take heed'(16:90). Four cardinal virtues may be taken out of this verse in a broad sense: justice, charity/benevolence (helping one another), chastity or modesty, and mercy.

JUSTICE

Islam is sometimes regarded as a religion of justice. Justice is perhaps the most important of the supreme values and cardinal virtues of Islam. It can be said that one of the main purposes of revelation and the tasks of prophets has been to establish justice in society. There are many verses about justice in the

Qur'an. In all their dealings, Muslims are required to stand firmly for justice even if it be against themselves or their kith and kin: 'O you who believe! Stand out firmly for justice, as witnesses to Allah, even though it be against yourselves, or your parents, or your kindred, and whether it be against rich or poor, for Allah is nearer to both (than you are)' (4:135).

Justice is the first principle of social life. It can be shown to govern all relations in life; between ruler and ruled, rich and poor, husband and wife, parents and children. Muslims have to be just even with those who they hate, as God has said in the Qur'an: 'O you who believe! Be steadfast witnesses for Allah in equity; and let not hatred of any people make you swerve from justice. Deal justly; that is nearer to Godfearing' (5:8).

CHARITY

Charitableness, helpfulness, helping one's kith and kin, concern for neighbours, assisting the weak and oppressed, and nursing the sick are all activities that are highly valued in Islamic ethics. Islam teaches that we are all equally creatures of God, all sharing the same condition. The Muslim's obligation is to live in cooperation, not competition, with his fellow men and to be helpful, kind, just and compassionate towards everyone, regardless of whether they are of the same or a different faith, race, culture or status. Among the many things that can contribute towards social justice, peace and harmony in society is the virtue of helping each other especially in matters of goodness and piety. The Qur'an exhorts us to: 'Help one another in goodness and piety, and help not one another in sin and transgression'(5:2).

Charity does not consist merely of offering help to the needy; rather it includes anything one does which is of good to others. A *hadith* of the Prophet mentions that charity includes removing thorns from the road and smiling at one's brother. And open-handedness in spending and giving are to be practised not only towards the poor but also towards one's family, relatives, friends, neighbours, guests and even strangers. Generosity and hospitality are thus highly valued qualities among Muslims in every part of the world. Allah's command to help each other in goodness is not only limited to Muslims, but it covers the whole of mankind in matters that bring virtue to all human beings. This is in line with the verse in the Qur'an: 'Allah does not forbid you to be kind and equitable to those who have neither made war on your religion nor driven you from your homes. Allah loves the equitable' (60:8). People who do not help one another are criticised and warned in the Qur'an:

> No! But you do not honour the orphan. Nor do you urge one another to feed the needy. Rather, you devour the inheritance (*of the orphan*) unsparingly. And you love wealth with an exceeding love. No! But when the earth is crushed to fine dust, and your Lord comes with

angels, rank upon rank, and Hell is brought near, on that day man will remember. But what will remembrance avail him? He will say: Would that I had done good works in my life! (89:17–24)

MODESTY

Modesty or chastity is also an important virtue in the Islamic system of morality for all Muslims, men or women. To the true Muslim, man and woman alike, anything impure or degrading is abhorrent and to be avoided. Strict modesty of dress, manner and behaviour, and absolute chastity are required both before and after marriage. The most famous personal example of chastity in the Qur'an is the Virgin Mary: 'And (*remember that blessed woman*) who guarded her chastity' (21:91).

The virtue of chastity is required or recommended equally to men and women in the Qur'an: 'And let those who cannot find a way to marriage be chaste until Allah of His bounty enrich them' (24:33). Both men and women are praised for their virtue of chastity or modesty in the Qur'an:

Behold; men who surrender to Allah, and women who surrender, and men who believe and women who believe, and men who obey and women who obey, and men who speak the truth and women who speak the truth, and men who persevere (*in righteousness*) and women who persevere, and men who are humble and women who are humble, and men who give alms and women who give alms, and men who fast and women who fast, and men who guard their modesty and women who guard (*their modesty*), and men who remember Allah much and women who remember, Allah has prepared for them forgiveness and a vast reward. (33:35)

MERCY

An entire chapter in the Qur'an is named after Allah's divine attribute *Ar-Rahman*, or 'The Most Gracious'. Also two of Allah's attributes are derived from the word for mercy. They are *Ar-Rahman* and *Ar-Rahim*, which mean 'The Most Gracious' and 'The Most Merciful'. These two attributes are mentioned in the phrase recited at the beginning of 113 chapters of the Qur'an: 'In the name of Allah, the Most Gracious, the Most Merciful.' This phrase is a continuous reminder for the reader of Allah's endless mercy and great bounties. Allah assures Muslims in the Qur'an that whoever commits a sin will be forgiven if he repents and ceases this act, provided that he says what means: 'Your Lord has prescribed for Himself mercy, that whoso of you does evil and repents afterward and does right, (*for him*) assuredly Allah is Forgiving, Merciful' (6:54).

The total objective of the Prophet's mission, as was described to him by Allah in the Qur'an, is mercy: '(O Muhammad!) We have only sent you as a mercy for all worlds' (21:107). Therefore, it is possible to conclude that mercy is one of the most essential Islamic virtues and anything which conflicts with mercy does not coincide with the Prophet's mission. Mercy and forgiveness even seem to be more supreme moral virtues than the most essential virtue of justice. It is said in the Qur'an that 'The recompense of an ill-deed is an ill-deed thereof. But whosoever pardons and seeks reconciliation, his reward is with Allah. Lo! He does not love the wrong-doers' (42:40).

The Islamic concept of mercy starts with God and is bestowed by Him to every living creature. Animals and humans alike show each other mercy, to live harmoniously with one another, and in turn, by showing this mercy, they themselves are shown even more mercy by Allah. Mercy encompasses kindness to animals as well as to humans, for abuse or cruelty of any of God's creatures is abhorrent to their creator. Such virtues are stressed again and again in the Qur'an and in the Prophet's sayings, as in the following hadith, for example: 'God will not show mercy to him who does not show mercy to others.' Mercy in Islam also extends to enemies. Evil is to be repelled with what is best. For example, wrath should be repelled with patience and endurance, ignorance with tolerance and persuasion, and evil with mercy and forgiveness. It is pointed out and recommended in the Qur'an that: 'Good and evil deeds are not equal. Repel evil with what is better; you will see that he with whom you had enmity has become your dearest friend' (41:34).

DAILY LIFE OF A MUSLIM

Birth

The Qur'an does not prescribe any rites connected with birth or the first period of life, but there are certain customs that Muslims should follow. When a child is born in a Muslim family, after the midwife has completed her task, the *adhaan*, or Call to the Prayer, is pronounced in the child's right ear and the *iqaamah*, or the establishment of prayer, in the left one, so that the first thing the child hears is the attestation of faith and the call to worship its creator.

Early Life

When the child's hair is cut for the first time, the weight of the hair in silver or its equivalent in current money is distributed among the poor. If the family has the means, a sheep or a goat is also sacrificed to entertain the poor and friends. This is called *aqeeqa* (sacrifice). No age limit is fixed, yet circumcision is practised on a male child at an early age.

After Puberty

When a child reaches the age of puberty, fasting during the month of Ramadan and daily prayers become obligatory. In Muslim families who practise properly, the child gets accustomed to them earlier.

General Habits

It is recommended that Muslims should say *Bismil-laah* (in the name of God) when commencing any action and *alhamdulil-laah* (thank God) after terminating it. When something is intended or promised for the future, they should immediately say *insha-allaah* (if God be willing). When two Muslims meet, they greet by saying *Salaam 'alaikum*. One can reply likewise, or say *Wa 'alaiku-mus-salaam*.

Food and Drink

All wholesome and good things are allowed to be used as food. As a general rule, all food is lawful unless it is declared *haram* (unlawful). All forms of pork and its by-products, as well as meat from carnivorous animals are specifically forbidden. Moreover, an animal whose meat is otherwise lawful becomes unlawful if it is not killed ritually. According to Islamic law, the animal should be killed in such a way that blood flows out and the name of God should be invoked while it is being killed. With regard to drink, Islam prohibits all kinds of alcoholic drink, but permits all varieties of soft drink.

Dress

Islam has not prescribed any particular dress and so Muslims enjoy a great variety of styles and fabrics. Seductive clothing may not be worn by either women or men, nor may they wear clothing inappropriate to their sex. Both men and women are expected to dress in a way that is modest and dignified.

Marriage

Children rarely leave home until the time they marry. The peace and security offered by a stable marriage and family unit is greatly valued in Islam. For the Prophet Muhammad said that, 'Young men, those of you who can support a wife should marry, for it keeps you from looking at strange women and preserves you from immorality' (al-Bukhari and Muslim). No Muslim girl can be forced by her parents to marry against her will. A Muslim marriage is a simple, legal agreement in which either partner is free to include conditions. A marriage dowry is given by the groom to the bride for her own personal use and she may keep her own family name rather than taking her husband's. Marriage customs vary widely from country to country.

There is a misconception concerning marriage in Islam; some people think that polygamy is the common form of Islamic marriage and 'all Muslims have four wives'. Whereas, in the whole of contemporary Islamic society, monogamy is the norm and polygamy is the exception. Polygamy, in Islam, is not an imposed and universal form of marriage. It is a divine concession to the distressing reality of social disasters, such as war and the surplus of women it creates, and other circumstances, such as the chronic sickness of the first wife. This can make polygamy necessary and practicable as a prevention and solution of the social problems which these unfortunate events would otherwise create. When these circumstances do not exist, polygamy ceases to flourish and monogamy is, as now, the norm. Moreover, even in these conditions, there is a further requirement of equity or justice mentioned in the Qur'an: 'if you fear that you cannot deal justly (*with so many*), then one only' (4:3). Furthermore, we read in the same chapter of the Qur'an: 'You will never be able to deal equally between (*your*) wives, however much you may desire (*to do so*)' (4:129).

Although it is not forbidden as a last resort, divorce is not common. Islamic teaching strongly disapproves of divorce but recognises the existence of marital situations that are irreconcilable, and in such cases it stipulates provisions for divorce that protect the wife and do least harm to the family as a whole.

Old Age

The strain of caring for one's parents is considered an honour and a blessing, as well as an opportunity for great spiritual growth. God asks that we not only pray for our parents, but act with limitless compassion, remembering that when we were helpless children they preferred us to themselves. Mothers are particularly honoured: the Prophet taught that 'Paradise lies at the feet of mothers.' When they reach old age, Muslim parents are treated mercifully, with the same kindness and selflessness. The Qur'an says: 'If either or both of them attain old age with you, (show no sign of impatience, and) do not (even) say 'fie' to them; nor rebuke them, but speak kind words to them' (17:23, 24).

Death

A Muslim on his deathbed tries to pronounce the formula of the faith: 'There is no god but God, and Muhammad is the messenger of God.' People around the patient also help by repeating it to the person in his death pangs. The body of the dead person is washed and cleansed before burial. After enshrouding the dead body, a funeral prayer is celebrated. Muslims consider this one of the final services they can do for their relatives and an opportunity to remember their own brief existence here on earth. The grave is dug on a north–south axis, parallel to Mecca, in so far as this is practicable and the head of the dead is turned slightly to the right (west), so that it faces the Kaaba. The Prophet taught that three things can continue to help a person even after death: the charity that they gave, the knowledge that they taught and prayers on their behalf by a righteous child.

5

Spiritual Dimension:
Religious Experience and Sufi Spirituality

God is the creator not only of our bodies, but also of all our faculties, which are diverse and each capable of development. It is He who has given us the intuition, the moral conscience and the means we employ to guide us in the right path. The human spirit is capable of both good and evil inspirations.... It is our duty to try to distinguish between that which is celestial and worthy of following, and that which is diabolic and fit to be shunned.

Among other means of communication between man and God, which are at the disposal of man, the feeblest perhaps is a dream. According to the Prophet, good dreams are suggested by God and guide men in the right direction.

Another means is *ilqa* (literally, throwing something towards someone), a kind of auto-suggestion or intuition, a presentiment of solutions in the event of an impasse or insoluble or difficult problems.

There is also the *ilham*, which may be translated as 'Divine inspiration'. Things are suggested to the heart (mind) of a man whose soul is sufficiently developed in the moral virtues of justice, charity, disinterestedness, and benevolence to others....When someone devotes one's self to God and tries to forget one's self, there are moments when the state of the presence of God flashes like lightning, in which one understands without effort that which no other effort would have succeeded in making him aware. The human spirit is thus enlightened; and then there is a sentiment of conviction, contentment and realisation of truth. (Hamidullah, 1980:65–6)

A religious experience is an experience that the person who has it perceives as being religious. In other words, the person believes that a naturalistic explanation of the experience is insufficient and that it can be explained only in terms of religious doctrines and in relation to some supernatural beings.

Although there are many such phenomena of religious experience among Muslims, the very concept of religious experience is relatively new for Muslims and academic research on this subject seems to be quite rare so far. Mohammed Iqbal writes that, 'There is no doubt that the treatment of religious experience, as a source of Divine knowledge, however, is historically prior to the treatment of other regions of human experience for the same purpose' (1988:15).

It seems that it is possible and useful to divide the content of the concept of religious experience into two simple and distinguishable types according to the state of the person having the experience. One is the mystical religious experience, which is the deepest and most intense, and is experienced by a relative minority of human beings, like the Sufis in Islam. The other is ordinary and popular religious experience, which is relatively superficial and weaker, but is experienced by the majority of people.

RELIGIOUS EXPERIENCE

Religious experiences include many different kinds of personal and subjective experience, although the experiences of ordinary people were not usually recorded in books, at least not until recent times. So it is not easy to draw up a classification; nevertheless, in an attempt to do so, there are three main groups of experiences that are recognised amongst Muslims.

Experience of the Awareness of God in the Observation of the Creation

The Qur'an itself has several passages that describe the phenomena of nature as 'signs' of God: 'There are signs for believers in the heavens and in the earth' (45:3). It also says that, 'To Allah belongs the East and the West. Whichever way you turn, there is the face of Allah' (2:115). Thus, to reflect on the signs of God in the universe and to try to experience His face everywhere is a religious duty imposed by the Qur'an.

During the spiritual journey of Muslims, God is experienced first of all as the Creator and Sustainer of the universe. Man begins his journey to God in this world, which displays, in its existence, forms, harmony and laws, the Creator who bestowed existence upon it. The Muslim sees total obedience to God as the natural consequence of His being the Creator of the world as well as the Being who rules over the universe and whose will governs all things.

A different version of this kind of religious experience is an experience of 'the light of faith' in God reflected by a fellow believer. In this kind of experience, when looking at the face of an individual, someone might see in that face 'the light of faith' coming from God as a gracious gift. This seems to be a common experience among Muslims from the time of the Prophet to the present day. Sometimes, it occurs as the result of observing a certain trait in a pious man; while sitting and talking with the man, one feels a flash of light suddenly coming from him and striking one. At other times, it is caused by some personal circumstance. Once a Bedouin, who until that time had showed bitter enmity to the Prophet, came to him and when his eyes fell upon the brilliant face of the Prophet and saw the scintillating light of prophethood coming forth from it, he said, 'By God, this is not the face of a liar!' Then he asked the Prophet to tell him about Islam and became a Muslim.

Experience of God's Presence during Service to God or at any Time (ihsan)

In his celebrated exposition of his teaching on faith (*iman*), submission (*islam*) and the best method of submission, the Prophet Muhammad defined this last point in the following terms: 'As to the embellishment (*ihsan*) of conduct, so render your service unto God as if you see Him; even though you do not see Him, yet He sees you.'

It is essential to perform the rituals of Islam as if in the presence of God or, at least, with the awareness that God sees and knows not only a Muslim's actions but also his intentions. *Ihsan* thus guards against the danger of the religious practices provided by revelation becoming empty rituals. It also serves to remind Muslims that the presence of Allah is a reality. Therefore, it is necessary for Muslims to maintain the remembrance and awareness of Allah's presence in their hearts at all times. Of course, for some Muslims *ihsan* is just as a deepened intellectual understanding, while for others it as a strong religious experience as if they actually see God.

Experience of God's Help for a Good or Needy Person in a Miraculous Manner

This kind of experience is narrated both in historical works and in some contemporary ones. As a historical example, one may remember al-Ghazali's experience of the light which God shone into his breast when he underwent a spiritual crisis that transformed him utterly.

In his autobiographical book, *Deliverance from Error*, the eleventh-century theologian and mystic al-Ghazali writes that, when he was teaching students in Baghdad, where he held one of the most distinguished positions in the academic world of his day, he caught the 'disease' of scepticism. 'The disease was baffling, and lasted almost two months, during which I was a sceptic in fact though not in theory nor in outward expression. At length God cured me of the malady,' he writes. But what is important in this autobiographical tale is that al-Ghazali mentions that 'this did not come about by systematic demonstration or marshalled argument, but by a light which God most high cast into my breast. That light is the key to the greater part of knowledge'. Immediately after reporting his own personal religious experience, he reminds his reader that 'whoever thinks that the understanding of things Divine rests upon strict proofs has in his thought narrowed down the wideness of God's mercy' (al-Ghazali, 1953:25).

As for contemporary examples of this sort of religious experience, although they have not been a topic of academic research in Muslim countries, some of them can be classified as follows:

- A dream, usually with a religious content, that comes true within a short period of time.

- A child's intuition that comes true. For example, a child says to his mother that this or that building will be destroyed; this or that person will die soon. The mother does not believe it, but that night an earthquake happens and what the child said comes true.

- God's guidance in a dream. According to one story, an intellectual atheist and a young village boy discuss the creation of the universe in the context of God's existence. The atheist argues against the concept of creation and tries to explain it as a kind of natural formation, but he is also influenced by the boy's ideas. After the discussion they go to sleep and the atheist has a dream. He rises up to the sky and hears a voice saying '*al-Anbiyaa* thirty...*al-Anbiyaa* thirty...' Then he falls back to the earth and wakes up; but he remembers the voice. In the morning he asks the boy, who says that *al-Anbiyaa* is the name of a chapter, *surah*, in the Qur'an, and that the thirtieth verse should be looked at. The boy opens his Qur'an, finds *al-Anbiyaa* thirty, and they are surprised to see that it is about their discussion and, in particular, about the specific concern of the atheist: 'Do not the unbelievers see that the heavens and the earth were joined together (as one unit of creation), before We clove them asunder? We made from water every living thing. Will they not then believe?' (21:30).

- Resurrection of a dead person to help a needy one and then that person suddenly disappears. Someone talks to and helps a boy and his mother; after a few days, the father of the boy looks for the man to thank him but finds out that he had died about a month before.

- Being in two different places at once to help a needy person. In answer to the prayer of a poor woman, her husband comes back from the city where he works and gives her sufficient money, and afterwards he disappears. The woman phones his house in that distant city and finds out that he was there all the time.

- Power of prayer or curse. A girl in a difficult situation prays sincerely and afterwards her family suddenly change their minds and approve her desire to go to university. Having been cursed by a pious man, a cruel rich man loses his sons and wealth (Yaran, 2004a:11–2).

Although these and other sorts of experiences are not necessarily expected or even credulously believed by all Muslims, they are usually interpreted by the persons having the experience as being evidence of God's help, providence and mercy. Ordinary Muslims do not expect to have personal religious experience and are reluctant to speak about it; nevertheless, if and when they do have such experiences, they are of course very happy and consider them to be God's blessing, favour and gift to them, and their belief in God's presence, justice and mercy grows stronger in both heart and mind. Having personal religious experience is contradictory neither to believing in revelation (*wahy*) nor to having a sincere, religiously based faith in God. By contrast, it would support and strengthen an existent belief in God. It is a similar case to the Prophet Abraham's anecdote narrated in the Qur'an: 'When Abraham said: 'Show me, my Lord, how You give life to the deed!' He asked, 'Do you not believe?' Abraham answered, 'Yes indeed, I do believe; but I wish to set my heart at rest" (2:260).

In addition, as al-Ghazali points out, if someone is already a believer in God and really sincerely wants to have a more direct and deep religious experience, he or she has more chance to have it. If they want to be included within the travellers of the hereafter with God's grace as their friend, the doors of guidance are opened up to them while they remain engaged in actions attached to God-fear and restrain themselves from passions and lusts, and try to impose discipline and self-mortification. Through these efforts, a light from God will fall in their hearts as God says in the Qur'an (29:69): 'Whosoever strives for Us, We shall guide them in our paths, for God is assuredly with those who do right' (al-Ghazali, 1953:124).

When we look at the epistemological and evidential state of religious experience in Islam, it is not difficult to guess that a typical medieval mystic, a *sufi* for instance, and a typical medieval theologian, a *mutakallim* if you like, would answer in rather different ways.. For a typical sufi, personal religious experience is not, for example, one of the secondary and supportive grounds of faith, but the strongest and the most direct, reliable and desirable motive. For the thirteenth-century poet and Sufi mystic, Mawlana Jalal al-Din Rumi, love is the essence of all religion and religious experience. Not only is faith generated by love, but, what is more, faith generated by any other motive is almost worthless (see Iqbal 1983:259–61). This certainty is expressed in the following verse:

> Reason, explaining Love, can naught but flounder
> Like ass in mire: Love is Love's own expounder.
> Does not the sun himself the sun declare?
> Behold him! All the proof thou seek'st is there. (Rumi 1950, 43)

For a typical medieval theologian, on the other hand, personal religious experience does not mean very much in a properly based faith. Al-Maturidi (d. 944), for example, 'refutes the idea of those who think that the individual mind is the basis of knowledge and criterion of truth. He also does not regard inspiration (*ilham*) as a source of knowledge. Inspiration, he argues, creates chaos and conflicts in the domain of knowledge, makes true knowledge impossible, and is ultimately liable to lead humanity to disintegration and destruction for want of a common standard of judgement and universal basis for agreement' (Ali, 1963: 264).

But for a scholar like al-Ghazali, who is both mystic and theologian at the same time, both religious experiences and theistic arguments are sufficient and valuable grounds for a person's religious belief. The difference between them is not in essence but in degree. When considering the genuine and strong religious experience, al-Ghazali compares the way of immediate experience with the way of rational argumentation like this: 'What a difference between being acquainted with the definition of drunkenness... and being drunk. Indeed, the drunken man while in that condition does not know the definition of drunkenness nor the scientific account of it; he has not the very least scientific knowledge of it. The sober man, on the other hand, knows the definition of drunkenness and its basis, yet he is not drunk in the very least' (1953:55).

Although I mentioned Rumi and al-Maturidi as representing two opposite perspectives, it is important to clarify that Rumi does not reject rational belief nor does al-Maturidi deny experience and inspiration. As A. Iqbal says, 'Rumi admits the utility of the intellect and does not reject it altogether. His emphasis on intuition as against intellect is explained by the fact that some of his outstanding predecessors had placed an incredible premium on reason.... Rumi gives an important place to knowledge' (1963:261–3). On the other hand, as Ayyub Ali says, al-Maturidi was never a hard rationalist and 'always tried to adopt a middle course between the extreme Rationalists and the Traditionalists' (ibid.:264).

Thus, for a moderate evaluation from an Islamic perspective, one can say that religious experience seems to be sufficient grounds for a person's belief in God, particularly if it is in harmony with the essence of revelation and reason. For it seems that the religious experiences of millions and millions of individuals who have been aware of God's presence and guidance – to be cured of sceptical disease as in the case of al-Ghazali – or His help and providence – to be cured of physical diseases and the like – are more likely to be real and genuine experiences, in the sense of having a real object or source of experience, and it is much less likely that the great majority of people, including very intelligent men and women, have been deluded by various imaginary experiences or projections. Indeed, Badham writes that 'the primary religious figures were manifestly in touch with reality. What is impressive about the prophets is the soundness of their political and social judgements. On any reckoning, Jesus of Nazareth was at the very least a wise and perceptive teacher, and Muhammad was a brilliant general, statesman and lawgiver. Likewise, contemporary religious experience is associated with a high level of mental alertness and psychological stability.' 'To identify either prophetic or contemporary religious experience with mental disorder,' he concludes, 'would seem wholly unjustified' (Badham, 1998:131).

In addition to this, as Mohammad Iqbal states, 'The revealed and mystic literature of mankind bears ample testimony to the fact that religious experience has been too enduring and dominant in the history of mankind to be rejected as mere illusion.' There is no reason, according to him, 'to accept the normal level of human experience as fact and reject its other levels as mystical and emotional. The facts of religious experience are facts among other facts of human experience and, in the capacity of yielding knowledge by interpretation, one fact is as good as another (1988:16).

Having accepted that mystical experience of God's existence is a real and authentic experience, could it have an evidential value for non-mystics as well? In answer to this question, a number of different views have been argued by philosophers of religion. As examples of three different positions, it is worth mentioning that Matson's answer is 'negative' (1965:25), Hick's answer is neither negative nor positive – namely, he writes, 'the agnostic position must be accepted...' (1970:115) – and Swinburne's answer is positive. According to Swinburne, there is a basic principle of rationality, which he calls the principle of testimony, that 'those who do not have an experience of a certain type ought to believe any others when they say that they do – again, in the absence of evidence of deceit or delusion' (1996:133). The answer of Mohammad Iqbal seems to be completely positive provided that 'we are in possession of tests which do not differ from those applicable to other forms of knowledge.' He calls these tests 'the intellectual test and the pragmatic test'. By the intellectual test, he means, 'critical interpretation, without any presuppositions of human experience, generally with a view to discover whether our interpretation leads us ultimately to a reality of the same character as is revealed by religious experience.' 'The pragmatic test,' he affirms, 'judges it by its fruits' (1988:27).

One can conclude that the argument from various types of religious experience for the existence of God should be considered as sufficient evidential grounds for persons who do have that experience provided that he or she has no obvious doubt of being deceived or deluded by it, and that the experience had is in harmony, at least in its essence, with his or her more objectively sound background knowledge based on reason and/or revelation. The case of those who have not had a religious experience themselves is similar, in general, but different in the degree of evidential value. The evidential value of mystical religious experience for non-mystics should be much less than the mystics themselves. Nevertheless, for non-mystics, too, the extraordinary experiences of the mystics, accompanied and supported by their exceptionally high moral quality, excellent intellectual ability and sometimes unusual miraculous powers, require a satisfactory explanation. And the more likely and satisfactory explanation seems to be the presence and providential activity of God.

SUFI SPIRITUALITY

In Islamic teachings, as we have already seen, there are certain external duties, such as prayer, fasting, almsgiving and abstaining from evil and wickedness. There are also internal duties or rather the internal dimension of those external duties, such as gratitude to God, sincerity, devotion and freedom from egoism. Sufism or Islamic mysticism is a specific training for those who would like to improve this latter aspect of Islamic life. Muslim mystics are generally called Sufis. The Sufis have looked upon themselves as Muslims who take seriously God's call to perceive his presence both in the world and in the self. They tend to stress inwardness over outwardness, contemplation over action, spiritual development over legalism, and cultivation of the soul over social interaction. On the theological level, Sufis speak of God's mercy, gentleness and beauty far more than they discuss the wrath, severity and majesty that play important roles in both Islamic jurisprudence (*fiqh*) and Islamic dogmatic theology (*kalam*). Sufism has been associated both with specific institutions and individuals and with a rich literature (Chittick, 2003:19; 1995:103).

As Annemarie Schimmel points out, Sufism traces its origins back to the Prophet Muhammad and takes inspiration from the Qur'anic verses like 'Whichever way you turn, there is the face of Allah' (2:115; see also 50:16, 6:103, 5:59).

> God has put signs into nature and into the human soul (51:21), and it is necessary to see and to understand them. Muhammad is the first link in the spiritual chain of Sufism and his ascension through the heavens into the divine presence, to which the first lines of chapter 17 of the Qur'an allude, became the prototype of the mystic's spiritual ascension into the intimate presence of God. According to the tradition, esoteric wisdom was transmitted from Muhammad to his cousin and son-in-law 'Ali ibn Abi Tâlib, the fourth of the righteous caliphs (d. 661). Other members of his family and his friends were endowed with mystical insight or pursued mystical practices. (Schimmel, 1975:24–7)

Out of this nucleus of pious people around the Prophet Muhammad has emerged a definition that was adopted by the Sufis: that is, the threefold attitude of *islam, iman* and *ihsan. Ihsan* was added with the meaning 'that you worship God as if you see Him', for even though man does not see God, God always sees man. With the addition of this third element the complete interiorisation of Islam begins (Schimmel, 1975:29).

Ihsan, 'worshipping God as if one see Him', is not discussed by the most vocal of the scholars who speak for Islam, that is, the jurists (*fuquha'*). By self-definition they limit their field of vision to the Shariah, which defines the Five Pillars and the other practices that Muslims need to perform. Nor is it discussed by a second influential group of scholars, the theologians (*mutakallimun*), who are the experts in the science of kalam, or dogmatic theology. Their concern is to articulate and defend creedal teachings, which establish and explain the meaning of the principles of belief. Neither of these schools of thought has the interest or the competence – qua jurists and theologians – to deal with 'worshipping God as if one see Him', so we would be wasting our time if we read their books looking for an explanation. It is the Sufis who take doing what is beautiful as their own special domain (Chittick, 2003:4, 5; 1994, Part III).

The life of a Sufi, dervish or mystic begins with repentance for the past sins and the reparation, as far as possible, of the harms done to other people. It is only then that one can march on the path leading to the Lord. The provisions for this journey are twofold: obedience to God and constant remembering of Him.

Sufism has 'many of the characteristics of monasticism, but does not usually preach celibacy. It does enjoin mortification of the flesh, and exalts the ideal of poverty, but it includes ordinary members of society in its ranks, with no distinction of clerical versus lay. It emphasises the love of God and teaches that God and the Sufis have a special relationship.' Baldick also highlights that 'They are perpetually engaged in remembrance (*dhikr*) of Him. Sufism also constitutes a path (*tariqa*), which begins with repentance and leads through a number of "stations", representing virtues such as absolute trust in God, to a higher series of ecstatic "states"' (Baldick, 1989:3).

The Sufis are distinguished from other Muslims partly because they consider the remembrance of God, in the form of mentioning His names as instructed by their shaykhs, as incumbent, not merely recommended. By doing this they celebrate the Qur'anic verses: 'O you who believe! Remember Allah with much remembrance. And glorify Him early and late' (33:41–2). For them, the essence of all the ritual activities is remembering God. People should pray and fast to remember God, to keep Him constantly in mind. 'There is no god but God' is commonly called 'the best *dhikr*'. But some others hold that the single remembrance, the mention of the name *Allah* alone, is superior. The goal of remembering God is to annihilate everything other than God and to come to subsist in the divine.

Among other Sufi practices, one may mention a life of asceticism, self-mortification and meditation, particularly on death and the final judgement. These are not ends, but only the means, rather temporary and provisional, for the purpose of mastering and breaking the ego. Spiritual practices enhance certain faculties, yet the acquisition of such faculties, however miraculous they might be, is not the aim of one who travels towards God.

The Sufis view God as beloved and lover, and they desire closeness (*uns*) with him, the worshipper's relation to God, described by the Qur'an as 'nearer to him than the jugular vein' (50:15). Their main goal is to reach (recognition of the) oneness of God (*tawhid*), the love of God (*mahabbah*) and the gnosis of God (*ma'rifah*). In their spirituality or journey towards God they have many experiences, but it is possible to classify these into three main types. First and foremost are the various experiential states and stations, then there are experiences relating to the removal of the veil (*kashf*) of sensual perception, and finally the experience of miracles (*karamat*).

'STATES' AND 'STATIONS'

The Sufis came to represent asceticism, retirement from the world and devotion to divine worship. 'Then, they developed a particular kind of perception which comes about through ecstatic experience. ... The exertion and worship of the Sufi novice must lead to a 'state' that is the result of his exertion. That state may be a kind of divine worship. Then, it will be firmly rooted in the Sufi novice and become a 'station' for him' (Ibn Khaldun, 1958:77–8).

> They distinguished between *maqam,* ('station') and *hal* ('state'): State is something that descends from God into a man's heart, without his being able to repel it when it comes, or to attract it when it goes, by his own effort. The *maqam* is a lasting stage, which man reaches, to a certain extent, by his own striving. It belongs to the category of acts, whereas the states are gifts of grace. The *maqamat,* ('stations') define the different stages the wayfarer has attained in his ascetic and moral discipline. He is expected to fulfill completely the obligations pertaining to the respective stations: e.g., he must not act in the station of respect as if he were still in the station of repentance; he also must not leave the station in which he dwells before having completed all its requirements. (Schimmel, 1975:99–100)

There are many ways in which Sufis have described these experiential steps leading from man to God. Especially in the case of the states, it is hardly possible to limit them to a set number. In one of the earliest authoritative texts of Sufism, Abu Nasr al-Sarraj (d. 988) enumerates ten states of the soul: constant attention (*muraqabah*), proximity to God (*qurb*), love (*mahabbah*), fear (*khawf*), hope (*raja*), spiritual yearning (*shawq*), familiarity (*uns*), tranquillity (*itmi'nan*), contemplation (*mushahadah*) and certainty (*yaqin*). Likewise, one of the earliest and finest accounts of the stations in Sufism is the *Maqamat-i arba'in* ('Forty Stations') by the eleventh-century Sufi master Abu Sa'id ibn Abi'l-Khayr. He numbers these as intention, conversion, repentance, discipleship, spiritual struggle, patience, invocation, contentment, opposition to the carnal soul, agreement, surrender, confidence, asceticism, worship, abstention, sincerity, truthfulness, fear, hope, annihilation, subsistence, the science of certainty, the truth of certainty, gnosis, effort, sanctity, love, ecstasy, proximity, meditation, union, unveiling, service, catharsis, aloneness, expansion, the ascertaining of the Truth, the supreme goal, and the fortieth is Sufism in its real sense (Nasr, 1991:76–81).

The Sufi continues to 'progress from station to station, until he reaches the (recognition of the) oneness of God (*tawhid*) and the gnosis (*ma'rifah*) which is the desired goal of happiness. ... Thus, the Sufi must progress by such stages. The basis of every stage is obedience and sincerity. Faith precedes and accompanies all of them. Their result and fruit are states and attributes. They lead to others, and again others, up to the station of the (recognition of the) oneness of God and of gnosis (*'irfan*)' (Ibn Khaldun, 1958:78). One of the most important of these stations is annihilation (*fana*) in God. The Sufi goal is annihilation (*fana*) in Allah, which transforms the individual ego to become an instrument of the divine purpose in the world (*baqa*). To be sure, *tawhid*, understood in the sense of realisation of oneness with God, has been regarded by many Sufis as the ultimate stage of Sufism. But the other view, that *tawhid* is only a stage of the Sufi *suluk* and that the final stage is servanthood (*'ubudiyah*) and the ultimate truth is difference (*baqa*) rather than oneness, union, or unification (*fana, jam, ijtihad*), has also been maintained by many other eminent Sufis (Ansari, 1986:45–6).

In a life of sincere obedience to the will of God, guided by the word of God, the life of His Prophet and the example of His saints, the Sufi is himself the recipient of such marks of favour as God may choose to vouchsafe him. Passing through the various states and stages of the spiritual pilgrimage, he encounters many proofs of the special relationship in which he stands to God. So guided and favoured, the Muslim mystic may hope to experience the removal of the veil (*kashf*) of sensual perception.

REMOVAL OF THE VEIL (*KASHF*)

States and stations are followed by the removal of the veil (*kashf*) of sensual perception.

> The Sufi beholds divine worlds which a person subject to the senses cannot perceive at all. The spirit belongs to those worlds. ... When the spirit turns from external sense perception to inner (perception), the senses weaken, and the spirit grows strong. It gains predominance and a new growth. The [remembrance] *dhikr* exercise helps to bring that about. It is like food to make the spirit grow. The spirit continues to grow and to increase. It had been knowledge. Now, it becomes vision. The veil of sensual perception is removed and the soul realises its essential existence. This is identical with perception. (The spirit) now is ready for the holy gifts, for the sciences of the divine presence, and for the outpourings of the Deity. Its existence realises its own true character and draws close to the highest sphere, the sphere of the angels. The removal of (the veil) often happens to people who exert themselves (in mystical exercise). They perceive the realities of existence as no one else (does) (Ibn Khaldun, 1958:81).

They like quoting the Qur'anic verse saying: 'As for those who strive in Us, We surely guide them to Our paths; and verily Allah is with the good' (29:26).

The removal of the veil *(kashf)* constitutes the epistemological side of the Sufi religious experience. According to al-Ghazali, God could not be known through rational discourse or speculation, as the philosophers had claimed or through union with him, as al-Bistami (d. 875) and al-Hallaj (d. 922) had claimed. Rather, He could be known through His self-unveiling *(kashf)* in the wake of an arduous and personal process of constant observation *(mushahadah)*; that is, through the effulgence of the divine light (Fakhry, 1997:78). Similarly, Ibn al-'Arabi asserts that 'unveiling is a mode of knowledge superior to reason, but he also insists that reason provides the indispensable checks and balances without which it is impossible to differentiate among divine, angelic, psychic, and satanic inrushes of imaginal knowledge' (Chittick, 1995:105).

> It is told that when the Prophet was taken on his *mi'raj* into the imme-diate presence of God, the angel Gabriel had to remain at the *sidrat-i muntaha*, 'the lotus tree of the farthest distance', because he can reach only the borders of the created universe, while the loving heart can enter the presence of God. So in Sufi tradition and particularly under the influence of Rumi, Gabriel is equated with the leading intellect which can bring the Prophet Muhammad and everyone who follows him to the borders of this universe, but only love [and the removal of the veil] can take the seeker further. (Schimmel, 2000:131–2)

Sufi metaphysics and ontology are based on this epistemology of *kashf*. 'The goal and fruit of this type of knowledge is commonly explained by citing the Prophet's saying, 'He who knows *[arafa]* himself knows his Lord.' As the *hadith* suggests, this sort of knowledge demands a simultaneous acquisi-tion of both self-knowledge and God-knowledge. The texts tell us repeat-edly that it cannot be found in books. Rather, it is already present in the heart, but it is hidden deep beneath the dross of ignorance, forgetfulness, outwardly oriented activity and rational articulation. Access to this knowl-edge comes only by following the path that leads to human perfection' (Chittick, 2003:32).

Among the Sufis, monistic and dualistic concepts of the relationship of Allah to his creation are known respectively as *wahdat al-wujud* (the unity of existence) and *wahdat al-shuhud* (the unity of experience). The unity of existence *(wahdat al-wujud)*, upheld mainly by followers of Ibn al-'Arabi, conceived of God as emanating the creation from Himself as a self-manifest-ation. Despite Ibn al-'Arabi's note that there is an unbridgeable distinction between the *Rabb* (Lord) and the *'abd* (servant), his position tends towards monism. According to the unity of experience or *wahdat al-shuhud*, it is asserted, for example by Shaykh Ahmad Sirhindi, that there is something other than God which exists. Against the background of this 'negative' material, we can clearly see God's positive attributes reflected in the world. Once we grasp the fact that we are not dealing here with a philosophical or theological system, we can begin to appreciate the difficulty of providing even an elementary understanding of *wahdat al-wujud* and *wahdat al-shuhud*. As Ibn Khaldun points out, 'competent recent Sufis say that during the removal (of the veil), the Sufi novice often has a feeling of the oneness (of existence). Sufis call that the station of 'combination' (*jam'*). But then, he progresses to distinguishing between existent things. That is considered by the Sufis the station of 'differentiation' (*farq*). That is the station of the competent gnostic' (1958:91).

SUFI MIRACLES (*KARAMAT*)

All the Sufis are agreed in affirming the miracles (*karamat*) of the saints, such as walking on water, talking with beasts, travelling from one place to another, or producing an object in another place or at another time. All these examples are duly recorded in the stories and traditions, and they are also spoken of in the Sufi literature. Such things happened both in the time of the Prophet and at other periods. For example, after the death of the Prophet, this happened to 'Umar ibn al-Khattab, when he called Sariyah, saying, 'O Sariyah ibn Hisn, the mountain, the mountain!' 'Umar was then at Medina in the pulpit and Sariyah was facing the enemy, a month's journey away. This story is well authenticated (al-Kalabadhi, 1979:57).

> One factor that led people to believe in the spiritual capacity of a Sufi leader was his ability to work miracles. ... There is no doubt that many Sufis indeed had extraordinary powers to perform acts that seemed to supersede natural laws. ... Innumerable stories are told about a shaykh's insight into his disciple's heart; he was able to tell his secret wishes, hopes and dislikes, to understand signs of spiritual pride or hypocrisy the very moment the adept entered his presence. ... The saint was able to disappear from sight, to become completely invisible and to practise *burūz*, exteriorisation, i.e., he could be present at different places at the same time. According to legend, Rumi attended seventeen parties at one time and wrote a poem at each one! The saint was capable of coming to the aid of his disciples wherever they were through the faculty of *tayy al-makan,* of being beyond spatial restriction, which is often attested to in hagiography. In cases of danger the shaykh might suddenly appear in the midst of a band of robbers to drive them away or assume the shape of the ruler in order to protect a disciple who called for help. ... Many miracles point to the capacity of the Sufi saint to spread the true Islamic doctrines. Even as a baby he will not drink his mother's milk in the daytime during the month of Ramadan, but only after sunset. In the desert

he is provided with facilities to perform his ablutions correctly. That illnesses are cured by means of religious formulae is well known – the story of the deaf girl who was cured by the saint's whispering the call to prayer into her ear is only one example from a long list of miracles in which the Sufis used prayer and *dhikr* formulae for healing purposes (Schimmel, 1975:205, 208).

It is claimed that the Sufis can sometimes foretell future happenings with God's allowance. According to a popular example of a miraculous experience of perceiving a future happening in medieval times, the authenticity of which cannot be determined however, a traditionalist named Molla Kasım decided to destroy the transcriptions belonging to the Sufi poet, Yunus Emre. Having stolen all of the poems, Molla Kasım sat on a river bank and started tearing up all the ones he found heretical, and throwing them into the river. After having destroyed about two thirds, he caught sight of a poem whose last couplet contained Yunus Emre's prediction about Molla Kasım. In the couplet, Yunus Emre had cautioned himself:

> Dervish Yunus, utter no word that is not true:
> For a Molla Kasım will come to cross-examine you.

When Molla Kasım read this prediction, he realised the greatness of Yunus and he immediately stopped destroying the poems (Halman, 1991:12). The legend of Lalla Mîmünah in the Maghreb is another example. She was a poor black woman who asked the captain of a boat to teach her the ritual prayer, but she could not remember the formula correctly. To learn it once more, she ran behind the departing boat, walking on the water. Her only prayer was: 'Mîmünah knows God, and God knows Mîmünah.' She became a saint and was greatly venerated in North Africa (Schimmel, 1975:430).

There was, however, one problem behind all the miracle stories that so delighted the crowds.

> To what extent was it legitimate for a mystic to perform miracles at all? The theologians carefully discussed the theories of miracles: the saint's miracles are called *karamat* (charismata) whereas the Prophet's miracles are classified as *mu'jizat,* 'what renders others incapable of doing the same', and the two types must never be confused. The general term for anything extraordinary is *khariq ul-adda,* 'what tears the custom' (of God); i.e., when God wants to disrupt the chain of cause and effect to which we are accustomed. The mystics have also argued, in lengthy deliberations, about whether miracles are performed in the state of sobriety or in that of mystical intoxication. They have classified the miracles under different headings... and whole collections have been composed to show the various kinds of miracles performed by Muslim saints (Schimmel, 1975:206).

It is important to realise that miracles are not performed by the Sufis for their own sake. 'The great Sufis do not think much of the removal (of the veil) and of activity among the low existentia. They give no information about the reality of anything they have not been ordered to discuss. They consider it a tribulation when things of that sort happen to them, and try to escape them whenever they afflict them' (Ibn Khaldun, 1958:81). Nevertheless, some of them point out that, as marvels (*mu'jizat*) were vouchsafed in the time of the Prophet in order to testify to the truth of his claim, so miracles (*karamat*) have happened at other periods for a similar reason. A true saint agrees with the Prophet both in words and mission; and the very appearance of miraculous powers in him only reinforces the Prophet and manifests his claim, strengthening his proof and right to be accepted in his mission and claim to be a Prophet; it also affirms the principle that God is One (al-Kalabadhi, 1979:57–9).

6

Contemporary Dimension:
Modern and Postmodern Issues

RATIONALITY AND SCIENCE

Islam places knowledge at the highest level of human endeavour. Repeatedly the Qur'an and the sayings of the Prophet urge the acquisition of knowledge. Indeed, the word knowledge, *'ilm,* is the most used after the name of God in the Qur'an. The Prophet urged his followers to 'seek knowledge, even unto China'. In the Qur'an, people are asked to think of and marvel at the variety confronting them: 'And of His signs is the creation of the heavens and the earth, and the difference of your languages and colours. Lo! herein indeed are portents for men of knowledge' (30:22). Islam also gives much importance to reasoning. In addition to many verses which exalt the capacity of reasoning, the following discourse between the Prophet and Muadh ibn Jabal, a judge on his way to the Yemen, clearly indicates the place and significance of rationality or reasoning:

> *Prophet:* How will you decide a problem?
> *Muadh:* According to the Qur'an.
> *Prophet:* If it is not in it?
> *Muadh:* According to the *sunna.*
> *Prophet:* If it is not in that either?
> *Muadh:* Then I will use my own reasoning.

The Prophet was so delighted at this reply that far from reproaching him he exclaimed: 'Praise be to God who has guided the envoy of His envoy to what pleased the envoy of God!' (Abu Dawud) This individual effort of reason and common sense on the part of an honest and conscientious man is not only a means of developing rational thought, but also received the benediction of the Prophet.

Starting from the Qur'anic commands to observe, to consider and to reflect upon nature and history, and arising from the integrated concept of knowledge frequently exalted and advised in the Qur'an, the desire to acquire knowledge became a deep-seated yearning. The Prophet Muhammad had also encouraged this sort of enterprise saying that, 'Wisdom is the lost-property of the believer; wherever he should find it, he should recover it.' This movement for scientific knowledge and progress led by Muslims lasted for at least seven centuries (from 700 to 1400 CE); and especially between the ninth and the thirteenth centuries Islamic civilisation made major original contributions to the development of science. This glorious phase was followed by a period of relative inactivity and even decadence that lasted for more than three hundred years (1400–1750). There followed a period of considerable rethinking for the Muslim world before the Western colonial powers began to retransfer modern science back to Muslim countries in the eighteenth century. There is evidence of scientific activities with steady but relatively slow growth thereafter (Qurashi, 1995:240–3).

Science and religion now appear to engender more amicable and constructive interaction than ever before. In order to accomplish this goal, however, careful and well-informed interdisciplinary studies are needed. If a productive dialogue is to be generated between science and theology, the arena for their interaction is natural theology. Natural theology may be defined as the search for knowledge about God through the exercise of reason and science.

Islamic theology is abbreviated to *kalam*. The term *kalam*, which literally means 'speech' or 'word', is used in Arabic translations of the works of Greek philosophers as a rendering of the term *logos* in its various senses of 'word', 'reason' and 'argument'. The aims of *kalam*, which soon became a highly sophisticated dialectical system, were to defend the faith through rational argument, to still the doubts of believers and strengthen their belief.

It seems almost necessary to start the history of natural theology in Islam with the Qur'an, the revealed scripture of Islam. Because almost one third of the Qur'an is made up of verses that exhort individuals to look at and reflect on themselves, their biological nature, the happenings on earth and in the heavens, and on historical events. It is obvious that these verses suggest the ideas of order, purpose, providence and so on. In this context, one can say that the first and most comparable movement of natural theology in Islam may be found in the Mu'tazilite *kalam*. As a matter of fact, it was the Mu'tazilite who laid the foundations of this new science in the eighth century and made a lasting contribution to its development. They started their movement by adopting a rational attitude in relation to some theological questions, but when they reached the height of their power, they adopted an aggressive attitude towards their opponents. The orthodox Muslims opposed the Mu'tazilite movement from the very beginning and tried to refute their doctrines by the traditional method. Thus, in one sense, Muslim theology began as a reaction against the rationalistic school of the Mu'tazilite and only gradually developed into a complete science.

Later on, conflicting ideas and antagonistic attitudes created chaos and confusion in Muslim thought and shook the foundation of old ideas and traditional beliefs. The need for reconciliation based on the adoption of a middle course and a tolerant attitude was keenly felt. It was at this critical period in the tenth century that a Muslim theology appeared in three parts of the Muslim world, represented by three eminent scholars: al-Maturidi in Central Asia, al-Ash'ari in Iraq and al-Tahawi in Egypt. They all endeavoured to reconcile conflicting ideas and settle the theological problems of the time by adopting a system that would satisfy reason and conform to the general tenets of the Qur'an and the Sunnah. They exercised a profound and lasting influence on the subsequent development of Muslim philosophy and theology.

Following the lead of Abu al-Hasan al-Ash'ari, the theologians tried to use logic, the instrument of their enemies, in order to defend the truths of revelation. From the tenth century onwards, this defence became more subtle and systematic, reaching its height in the works of al-Juwayni (d. 1085). With his pupil, al-Ghazali, *kalam* took a new turn. Opposed as it was from the beginning to the school of the philosophers, it now began to employ the syllogistic method, intellectual (*'agli*) evidence and certain theses of the philosophers, thus laying the foundations of the school of philosophical *kalam* developed by the later theologians.

It is interesting to note here that the role of al-Ghazali in Islamic theology and that of Thomas Aquinas in Christian theology seem to be similar in their endeavours to bring natural theology closer to the revealed scriptural theology and to mould them together in a spirit of scriptural, natural and rational unity.

After Fakhr al-Din al-Razi (1149–1209), theological thought increased in volume, but its quality is usually held to have declined. One of the signs of this alleged decline is the lack of originality. Instead of fresh works like those of al-Juwayni and Fakhr al-Din ar-Razi, the theologians seem to have focused their efforts on the production of commentaries and super-commentaries and glosses on earlier works. Before the 1900s, however, signs of the 'new dawn' in Islamic theology started to appear with some eminent Muslim theologians who began to produce original and influential books again. During recent decades, the philosophy of religion has also started to stimulate debate in the faculties of Islamic theology in some Muslim countries, and the topic of the relationship between science and religion has been elaborated in more detail.

When Christianity first met modern science in the seventeenth century, the encounter was a friendly one. By the eighteenth century many scientists believed in a God who had designed the universe, but they no longer believed in a personal God. By the nineteenth century some scientists were hostile to religion. In the twentieth century the interaction of religion and science has taken many forms. Some people have defended traditional doctrines, others have abandoned the tradition, and still others have reformulated long-held concepts in the light of science. Today, some people in both camps, science and religion, are aggressively continuing the warfare, particularly on the topic of evolution. For others, conflict can be avoided if science and religion are strangers occupying separate domains at a safe distance from each other. The two kinds of inquiry offer complementary perspectives on the world, separate and independent from each other and not in conflict. However, many people today are seeking a more constructive dialogue and partnership (Barbour, 2000:xi, xii).

We have met similar approaches in the Islamic world concerning the same issue of the relationship between modern science and Islam. Some positivists and some religious conservatives advocate that there is a conflict between modern science and Islam, particularly on the topic of evolution, and side in favour of science and religion respectively. On the religious side, 'modern science is guided not by moral values but by naked materialism. Its emphasis on constant change is in contradiction to the immutable values of Islam and its claims to high achievement and total dependence on human reason amount to worship of humanity' (Hoodbhoy, 1995:16). In close similarity with the radical critiques of science by some Europeans, it is also argued that the development and application of a supposedly value-free science is the prime cause of the great problems faced by the world today, such as weapons of mass destruction, environmental degradation and global inequities in the distribution of wealth and power.

A second Muslim attitude has been to treat the requirements of science as essentially unrelated to the direct concerns of Islamic faith. 'Its adherents are satisfied with the vague belief that Islam and science are not in conflict but are disinclined to examine such issues too closely' (ibid.). From their point of view, the preoccupations of those who search for a positive dialogue between Islam and science are redundant and even harmful.

A third approach among Muslims has been to advocate an essential compatibility between the major teachings of Islam and certain laws of science, and to reinterpret either the theological doctrines or the scientific theories in order to reconcile faith and knowledge. This school of thought has a historical tradition going back to the rationalist theology and philosophy movements in Islam. In this reconciliationist and reconstructionist tradition, it is argued that the precise and clear words of God cannot be wrong, but also that the established truths of science are real. Therefore the only issue is to arrive at suitable interpretations wherever there is an apparent conflict between revealed truth and physical reality (ibid.).

Looking at the attitudes towards the theory of evolution will give a sufficient clue to the relationship between Islam and modern science. In the contemporary Muslim world attitudes towards the theory of evolution are especially mixed. While forbidden in a few Muslim countries, teaching of the theory of evolution is allowed in Turkey, Egypt, Iraq, Iran, Indonesia and several other countries. Nevertheless, it is still a lively topic of debate in many circles and therefore it is worth considering in a bit more detail.

First of all, it should be stated that the subject matter of the origination of creation in cosmological or biological terms is neither a matter of dogmatic belief for Muslims nor a matter of divine mystery which is closed to the human mind, looked at from the perspective of the Qur'anic revelation. By contrast, the Qur'an encourages us to search creation, and not only the current case of it, but also its origination and beginning. It does not just encourage this, but also shows the method for doing so. Indeed, it is said in a verse like this: 'See they not how Allah produces creation, then reproduces it? Say (O Muhammad): Travel in the land and see how Allah originated creation, then Allah brings forth the later growth' (29:19–20).

So, searching for the origination of creation in the universe and the earth is obviously encouraged, and particularly the use of the inductive method through travel and observation is recommended, rather than deductive inference, philosophical speculation or theological reflection. This verse also shows that the creation is not a brute fact that suddenly happened all at once; by contrast it has a history, having an origination and continuation, production and reproduction. In other words, it is a gradually evolving cosmic fact.

Therefore, although it is a matter of suspicion and uneasiness because of the notorious conflict between atheistically interpreted Darwinism and theistic religions, including Islam, the issue of the origination of creation and its continuation and evolution are issues that are not only legitimate but also encouraged from the Qur'anic point of view.

Second, it should also be stated that the concept of evolution, the theory of biological evolution, the Darwinian and Neo-Darwinian theory of evolution, the mechanisms of evolution and the atheistic interpretation and ideology of Darwinism should not be thought of as the same thing. At least three dimensions should be differentiated: the *fact* of evolution in general, the *mechanisms* of evolution in accordance with an evolutionary theory such as the Darwinian or Neo-Darwinian one, and the atheistic *ideology* based on the Darwinian theory. Each of these has different connections both with science and with religion. The only one that is obviously in conflict with any religion is the last one, the atheistic ideology asserting to be based on 'blind' evolution. But an ideology or ideologically interpreted scientific theories are not science as such at all, nor are they an objective philosophical outcome of scientific views on evolution. As a matter of fact, even Darwin himself was not an atheist. So, briefly speaking, the concept and theory of evolution should not be equated with the atheistic interpretation of some Neo-Darwinist scientists and philosophers. Considering the theory of evolution as being equal to or strongly supportive of atheism and materialism has often prevented theists or religious people from looking at it without prejudice.

In this case, it should, by contrast, be known and openly stated that the concept of evolution is not the monopoly of atheist Darwinists, nor is it even the monopoly of Darwin himself; however, his contribution is much greater than that made by others. Indeed, various forms of evolutionary ideas have been known and defended, for example, by Muslim scientists and scholars since the very early periods of Islamic thought and science. One need mention only some of their names. Al-Nazzam (d. 835 or 845), al-Jahız (d. 869), Ikhwan al-Safa (early 11th-century organisation), Ibn Miskawayh (d. 1035), Ibn Tufayl (d. 1183), Ibn al-'Arabi (d. 1240), Mawlana Jalal al-Din Rumi (d. 1273), Ibn Khaldun (d. 1406) and Sadr al-Din al-Shirazi (d. 1640) were some of the Muslim scholars who defended some sort of cosmic or biological evolutionary ideas before the nineteenth century. Looked at from the perspective of the three dimensions on evolution mentioned above, it is clear that none of these Muslims defended an atheistic ideology based on evolution or interpreted evolution atheistically; nevertheless, all of them defended creation through some sort of evolutionary mechanism which includes both similar and different factors in comparison to modern theories of evolution.

Therefore, research into the question of evolution and creation in the Qur'anic revelation has an Islamic historical tradition as well as a Qur'anic foundation, as we will see below. But this does not mean that there is an obvious theory of evolutionary creation in the Qur'an, nor that all Muslim scholars believe in an evolutionary creation. What it means is that we can start to explore this issue independently of any prejudice, which may stem either from a modern hostility between atheistic Darwinian ideology and theistic religions like Christianity and Islam, or from a traditional and popular belief in a sudden and special creationism and in the medieval view of a static universe, which may have been related to human interpretations and commentaries of the holy texts based on ancient mythologies. For what the Qur'anic revelation says about the issue is, of course, much more important from the Islamic perspective than an apparently modern idea of conflict and hostility between revelation and evolution or a pre-modern theological tradition concerning sudden, special and static creation.

When exploring the issues of creation, evolution and evolutionary creation from the Qur'anic perspective, it is interesting to note that a very short phrase repeated in a few verses in the Qur'an seems to play a key role. One of the verses in which it appears is: 'But His command, when He intends a thing, is only that he says unto it: Be! And it is' (36:82).

The important part of this verse is the phrase 'Be! And it is', which most Muslims are familiar with at the level of popular religious culture. It seems that this phrase alone may represent three different approaches to the question of creation or evolution. Its traditional and popular religious understanding emphasises the first part of the phrase, 'Be!', inclusive of the second part, 'it is', and interprets the second part as if it is 'it was' or 'it immediately happened', rather than 'it is'. Thus, most Muslims simply think that as soon as this divine command was given, the object of the command came into being all of a sudden, as it was, in its most perfect form. This is the traditional interpretation of the verse and is the most common concept of creation; more technically speaking, this is the creationist approach.

Although they do not claim such a specific reference to this verse, a second group may be categorised as those who emphasise the second part of the phrase, 'it is', that is to say, the way in which things come into being naturally and exclusively of the first part, 'Be!', that is, the divine command before the evolutionary processes start. These are the modern positivists, materialists and atheists, whether they are originally Muslim or non-Muslim. This is the view of atheistic evolution.

And a third group may be categorised as those who see and interpret both parts of the phrase together without reducing one to the other, 'Be! And it is'. For them, like the first group and unlike the second group, there is a divine command before the beginning of creation, and like the second group and unlike the first group, the creation after the divine command does not come into being all of a sudden in its full perfection, but just starts to be, and then evolves gradually in accordance with the divine guidance and natural laws. This is the idea of evolutionary creation or theistic evolution.

Now we should look at these three approaches in the light of the Qur'anic verses.

Sudden and Special Creation (Emphasis inclusively on 'Be!')

As we have already said, the traditional and general understanding of God's act of creation in the Muslim mind seems to stem essentially from a commentary on a repeated phrase, as in the following verses from the Qur'an: '...when He decrees a thing, He merely says "Be!" – and it is.' (2:117); or 'The only word We say to a thing when We decree it, is that We say to it "Be", and it is.' (16:40). According to a common commentary on this verse, Allah's 'word' is itself the deed, the Truth. 'There is no interposition of Time or Condition between His Will and its consequences, for He is the Ultimate Reality. He is independent of the proximate or material causes, for He Himself creates them and establishes their Laws as He pleases' (*The Holy Qur'an with English Translation*, commentary on 16:40).

The same phrase is also used in the context of the way in which God determines a matter, or He intends a thing as well as He decrees or wills a matter: '...When He determines a matter, He only says to it, "Be!", and it is' (Qur'an, 19:35; cf. 36:82). According to a commentary on these verses, God's 'creation is not dependent on time, or instruments or means, or any conditions whatsoever. Existence waits on His Will, or Plan, or Intention. The moment He wills a thing, it becomes His Word or Command, and the thing forthwith comes into existence' (*The Holy Qur'an: English Translation of the Meanings and Commentary*, commentary on 38:82).

The same phrase is again used in connection with life and death: 'It is He Who ordains Life and Death. When He decrees a thing, He only says: Be! and it is' (Qur'an, 40:68). Commentaries on this verse reflect the same understanding, namely, an emphasis on the first part of the phrase, or an interpretation of the second part, 'it is', as if it was 'it was' rather than 'it is'.

According to a commentary, 'The keys of life and death are in Allah's hands. But He is not dependent on time or place or instruments or materials. All that He has to do is to say "Be", and it comes into existence' (*The Holy Qur'an: English Translation of the Meanings and Commentary*, commentary on 40:68).

Although this is a common commentary, is it really a true commentary or a coherent interpretation of God's acts when looked at from the Qur'anic perspective, and not from a theological or philosophical one? It seems that it is not. It may seem to be true from the perspective of rational or philosophical theology, but not from the perspective of revealed theology in the Qur'an.

From the perspective of philosophical theology, it is reasonable to suppose that since God is an omnipotent being, He can instantaneously do whatever He wants independently of time, place, instruments or materials – as some commentators say above. Indeed, one commentator states the very concept of philosophy using this interpretation: 'While in the life of created things there is "proportion and measure", and a lag of time or distance or circumstance, in Allah's command, the Design, the Word, the Execution, and the Consequences are but a single Act.... In Allah's Command, the word "Be" (*kun*) includes everything, without the intervention of or dependence on any other being or thing whatever. And this is also another phase of the philosophy of Unity' (ibid., commentary on 54:50).

However, if we do not misunderstand the Qur'an, it does not make such a claim, such a creation independent of everything such as time, space and materials. Instead, on the contrary, it clearly mentions various expressions of time (six, four, two days of creation), various places (the creation on earth), instruments (Allah sends the winds and they raise the clouds, etc.) and physico-chemical materials (creation from water, mud, dust, clay, etc.). Therefore, in terms of the Qur'an itself, the creation does not seem to be a matter of coming into existence all at once, without any time, matter and secondary causes and laws. So the instantaneously creationist approach, mainly based on the command 'Be!' (*kun*), does not seem to be the most appropriate representation of God's creationary act, although it is a common and traditional belief among Muslims. We will deal with this issue in the third subsection below and give evidence there to show that it seems to be a misinterpretation.

In addition to this, there does not seem to be a strong theological reason to believe that an Omnipotent's command and act has to become true all of a sudden, in its full excellence, particularly if we are taught this by the holy books, namely the Holy Qur'an for Muslims. Although this philosophical theology or intellectual expectation concerning God's command and act is understandable to some extent, it is in fact a similar expectation to that proposed by some unbelievers of Mecca when they argued that God must send down the Qur'anic revelation instantaneously in its full completeness.

Indeed, according to a verse in the Qur'an, 'those who disbelieve say: "If only the Qur'an would be sent down upon him all at one time!"' (25:32). For them this would be a more appropriate act for an omnipotent and omniscient God. However, as everybody knows, God did not do this and instead he revealed the Qur'an over a period of twenty-three years, explaining the reason as follows: 'Thus do We establish your heart with it and We have recited it in a distinct recitation' (25:32). If there is a process in the divine construction of the Qur'an, why should there not be a similar process in the construction of the universe or living beings? If it does not contradict the omnipotence of God, why should the creation of the universe as an evolving process contradict the Qur'an?

Atheistic Evolution (Emphasis exclusively on 'It is')

As we have already said, although they do not claim such a specific refer ence to this verse, a second group, or rather some modern Muslims and members of other religious groups, may be categorised as those who exclusively emphasise the second part of the phrase mentioned above. They choose to emphasise 'it is', that is to say the way in which things come into existence naturally, and virtually ignore the first part, 'Be', the divine command before the evolutionary process of creation. These are the modern positivists, materialists and atheists. For them, the physical cosmos and biological complexities and consciousness can be sufficiently explained just by natural causes and coincidences, such as mechanisms of natural selection based on genetic mutations, without recourse to any supernatural agency or transcendent being.

It would be superfluous to point out that this idea, or rather ideology, is completely wrong from the Qur'anic perspective. The Qur'an criticises the defenders of this idea for failing to think deeply enough in order to see the Creator behind the creation and asks them to think about the efficient and material causes of the cosmos and themselves: '… were they created out of the void? Or were they their own creators? Or did they create the heavens and the earth? Surely, they have no faith!' (52:35–6).

In another verse, the Qur'an cites examples of natural phenomena, for which some simple and secondary natural causes are known to us, and insists that being the cause of something is not the same as being the creator of that thing; likewise, knowing some occasional causes is not the same as knowing the whole cause and having a complete explanation. 'We created you: will you not believe? Behold (the semen) you emit: Do you create it or are We the Creator?' (56:57–9).

The Qur'an describes the creation of the universe phase by phase; nevertheless, it sees this explanation insufficient and draws attention to two essential and complementary questions: who did it and why? Without proper answers to these questions, any explanation will be insufficient and any belief will be wrong:

What! Are you harder to create than the heaven which *He* has built? *He* raised it high and fashioned it. *He* made dark its night and brought out its light. And after that *He* spread the earth, And then drew from it water and pastures. Then the mountains *He* fixed: A provision *for you* and for your cattle. (79:27–33)

So the atheistic evolution that does not have recourse to God as the transcendent ground or primary cause of the cosmos and consciousness, or in other words, an evolutionary view that does not see the divine command 'Be' behind the natural causes and processes of 'it is', is an insufficient and wrong belief from the Qur'anic perspective.

Evolutionary Creation or Theistic Evolution (Comprehension of 'Be! And it is' together)

As we have already mentioned, a third group may be categorised as those who see and interpret both parts of the phrase in the verse mentioned above as it is, without overemphasising or excluding either 'Be' or 'it is!'. In this understanding, there is a divine command before the beginning of creation and the creation that follows the divine command does not come into being all of a sudden, but just starts to be, evolving gradually in accordance with divine guidance and natural laws.

This is the idea behind evolutionary creation or theistic evolution. It seems that this is the most appropriate understanding both of the phrase in the Qur'an and of the concept of creation in Islam. For the Qur'an explains the creation over a gradual time, and involving some earthly matters in accordance with some natural causes, as well as giving the total explanation in terms of God's primary causality and activity in various ways. Let us look at these issues more closely.

1) *Phases of time in creation*

The Qur'an explains the creation of the heavens on various days, over long periods of time, and in many verses both in general and in relation to some particular physical beings. This verse, for example, describes how God's acts may take a long time: 'He directs the ordinance (*all affairs*) from the heaven unto the earth; then it ascends unto Him in a Day, whereof the measure is a thousand years of what you reckon' (32:5). In relation to the creation of more specific objects, the Qur'an often uses time expressions to mean very long periods or ages: 'And verily We created the heavens and the earth, and all that is between them, in six days…' (50:38; for similar verses, see also 7:54, 10:3, 25:59, 32:4, 57:4, 2:29).

As for the Creation in *six days*, in verse 22:47 we are told that a day in the sight of Allah is *like* a thousand years of our reckoning, and in verse 70:4 the comparison is with 50,000 of our years. Indeed, in the history of our material universe, we may reckon six great epochs of evolution. The Qur'an also explains some of the great changes that occurred in the heavens and on earth in a certain time: 'Do not the unbelievers see that the heavens and the earth were at first one piece, then We parted them...' (21:30).

Many contemporary religious Muslims are glad to see a close relationship between these sorts of verses and the Big Bang theory of creation. They have no serious objection to the Big Bang theory, which states that the physical universe came into existence through a singular explosion about 15 billion years ago, and the universe and life within it were constructed or evolved through a fine-tuned expansion from the beginning to the present time.

It is interesting to note that people who do not object to an evolving process in the inorganic realm have sometimes objected to such a process at an organic level. However, if we continue to read the Qur'an, we can see that living beings were also created gradually over a long period. For it is told in the Qur'an that '...We made every living thing from water' (21:30). That all life began in the water is a conclusion to which our latest knowledge in biological science points. According to a commentary on this verse, 'there is the fact that land animals, like the higher vertebrates, including man, show, in their embryological history, organs like those of fishes, indicating the watery origin of their original habitat' (*The Holy Qur'an: English Translation of the Meanings and Commentary*, commentary on 21:30).

Finally, humankind too was created over a long period of time. It is so long that it is not worth mentioning. The Qur'an asks clearly: 'Has there come over man a period of time when he was nothing, not mentioned?' (76:1). This verse is one of the most important verses from the perspective of evolutionary interpretation. In another, presumably better translation, this verse mentions 'a long period of time': 'Has there not been over man *a long period of time*, when *he was nothing* (not even) mentioned?' (*The Holy Qur'an: English Translation of the Meanings and Commentary*, commentary on 76:1). Although it is usually interpreted as being about man's development from a single sperm to birth and the period of gestation, some modern scholars interpret it as mentioning the long period of time passed in the evolutionary history of humankind before the first *Homo sapiens* or the first prophet, Adam. There is another important verse that supports the evolutionary interpretation above: '...it is He that has created you in *diverse stages*...' (Qur'an, 71:14).

Human creation and in particular the development of a foetus during the period of gestation are also described in the Qur'an as being gradual, phase by phase:

Man We did create from a quintessence (of clay); then We placed him as (a drop of) sperm in a place of rest, firmly fixed; then We made the sperm into a clot of congealed blood; then of that clot We made a (foetus) lump; then We made out of that lump bones and clothed the bones with flesh; then We developed out of it another creature. (23:12–14)

If the development of a foetus from sperm to a baby occurs phase by phase, why should not the creation of man 'from a quintessence of clay' occur phase by phase in a similar way through evolutionary processes? Indeed, the Qur'an clearly likens the two to each other: 'Your creation and your raising from the dead are only as the creation and the raising of a single soul' (31:28).

In addition, a verse uses the concept of beginning when it explains creation: 'Who made all things good which He created, and He began the creation of man from clay; Then He made his seed from an extract of despised water (*fluid*)' (32:7,8). It is interesting to note that the verse does not say that He created man from clay, but instead clearly states that 'He *began* the creation of man from clay'. This means that it did not happen in an instant, in the twinkling of an eye, but that it has a beginning, a development and further phases of perfection.

So it is quite obvious that God created the physical universe, the heavens and the earth, and all living beings, including humankind, over a gradual or evolving time, and not in a moment, hey presto! Moreover, every created thing seems to have an evolutionary history.

2) *Worldly matters used in creation*

God does not say that He created everything out of nothing. On the contrary, He mentions earth and many earthly matters or chemical elements, such as dead beings, water and clay, as the source materials used in the creation of human beings. For example, it is stated in the Qur'an that 'It is He who produced you from the earth' (11:61). In a similar verse, it is said that 'From (*the earth*) did We create you, to it shall We return you, and from it shall We bring you out once again' (20:55). The Qur'an also mentions some earthly matters in the same contexts. For example, it says about God that 'You bring forth the living from the dead and the dead from the living' (3:27; cf. 6:95, 10:31).

Many verses also single out the importance of water. In the Qur'an, God not only says that 'We made from water every living thing' (21:30), but other verses also give a clear explanation of the evolution of diverse species from water: 'And Allah has created every animal from water: Of them there are some that creep on their bellies; some that walk on two legs; and some that walk on four. ...' (24:45; cf. 21:30). Furthermore, the chemical matters of the human body are explained as various forms of water and dust: 'We created man of a clay of moulded mud. And the jinn did We create aforetime of flaming fire. And (remember) when your Lord said to the angels: 'I am creating man of a clay of moulded mud. When I shaped him and breathed My spirit into him, kneel down and prostrate yourselves before him!'' (15:26–9; cf. 38:71, 3:59, 37:11, 15:33, 55:14–15).

So, these verses show that the animate beings of the physical world were created by God out of worldly matter, and in the beginning, before the differentiation and evolution of species, using only one or at most two or three materials, like water.

3) *Natural causes or mechanisms in creation*

In the Qur'an, natural causes and the laws of natural events are never denied. By contrast, they are sometimes expressed with the intention of seeing both natural causes and laws and also the ultimate divine cause behind these causes and laws. For example, God describes some natural causes of rain, one after the other in this verse, after mentioning the first cause at the beginning: 'Allah is He who send the winds so that they raise (drive) clouds, and spreads them along the sky in the way He pleases, and causes them to break and you see the rain downpouring from within them' (30:48).

In a verse which is often used by evolutionary creationists, the Qur'an also uses some more insightful natural metaphors concerning the creation of human beings which associate some natural mechanisms of evolution: 'Allah has brought you forth from the earth like a plant' (71:17).

On earth, there is a struggle, conflict and even enmity between all creatures, including human beings. It is said in the Qur'an that 'Verily We have created man into toil and struggle' (90:4; cf. 2:36). As Mohammad Iqbal points out, 'this mutual conflict of opposing individualities is the world-pain which both illuminates and darkens the temporal career of life' (Iqbal, 1988:88). This struggle involves a natural selection; and the fittest, in terms of ability to adapt to the environmental conditions, will survive and evolve. It is one of the natural dynamics of the spiritual evolution of human beings, as well as biological one. But from the Qur'anic or religious perspective, the mechanisms of natural selection and mutations are not exclusively natural factors without any ultimate divine design behind them. It is said in the Qur'an that 'Your Lord creates what He wills and *chooses*....' (28:68). So, from the Qur'anic perspective, there is also a divine factor behind the natural mechanisms of evolutionary process, such as mutation and natural selection.

Looked at from the Qur'anic or even more holistic perspective, natural causes are required and effective, but they are not by themselves sufficient to explain the whole cause of the evolution of the cosmos and consciousness. There is also a divine cause and dimension to them. The divine cause first creates and then gives order, proportion, measure and guidance. This is stated in the Qur'an as follows: '...Who has created all things and well proportioned them; Who has ordained (their) destinies and guided (them)...' (87:2–3; cf. 20:50).

Four main divine influences are mentioned here in connection with creation. First, He brings us into being. Second, He endows us with forms and faculties exactly suited to what is expected of us and to the environments in which our life will be cast, giving to everything due order and proportion. Third, He has ordained laws and decrees, by which we can develop ourselves and fit ourselves into His whole scheme of evolution for all His creation. He has measured exactly the needs of all and given us instincts and physical predispositions which fit into His decrees. Fourth, He gives us guidance, so that we are not the sport of mechanical laws (*The Holy Qur'an: English Translation of the Meanings and Commentary*, commentary on 87:2–3). This guidance in its wider sense may be regarded 'as a principle of internal development of the species. To the lower animals have been given instincts and senses through which they are led on to balance and equilibrate themselves. And it is through seeing, hearing, feeling and smelling that they adapt themselves to their environment – and thus to sustain themselves and to procreate their species' (Brohi, 1988:84).

Within these essential dimensions of divine causation, God guides or directs some species, like human beings, to higher positions, while others stay at a certain point. Indeed, it is said in the Qur'an that 'He multiplies in creation what He pleases. For Allah is Able to do all things. That which Allah opens to mankind of mercy none can withhold it; and that which He withholds, none can release thereafter' (35:1–2; cf. 6:165). The same situation is clearly expressed in this verse, too: 'And had We willed, We verily could have *fixed* them in their place, making them *powerless to go forward or turn back*' (36:67).

So, as we have seen, together with divine causation, the Qur'an also mentions natural causes of evolutionary creation, as well as its worldly matters and worldly-like processes of time. Instead, what is rejected by the Qur'an is the possibility that natural causes are sufficient, independently of the divine cause behind or inside them.

4) *Teleology in creation and the evolution of souls and societies*

According to the Qur'an, the whole process of evolutionary creation is not a blind and purposeless phenomenon; by contrast, it is a teleological process in the sense of having a moral and spiritual aim that is the evolution of human souls and societies. It is said in the Qur'an that 'We did not create the heavens and earth, and all that is between them, in play. We did not create them except with truth; but most of them do not understand' (44:38–9). The zenith of this process is the evolution of souls and societies, and the most important purpose of creation and evolution is the development of individuals' good thoughts and actions towards each other, towards their environment and towards their creator. In this context, the Qur'an states, 'Who has created life and death that He may try you, which of you is best in conduct...' (67:2; cf. 6:165).

It seems, therefore, that – provided that the scientific theory of evolution is not equated with atheistically interpreted Neo-Darwinist ideology – the Holy Book of Islam is not inimical to the idea of evolution – provided also that its verses which 'are precise and clear in meaning' (Qur'an, 3:7) are not equated with human interpretations based mainly on ancient mythologies.

By contrast, seen from the perspective of many verses in the Qur'anic revelation, the concept of evolutionary creation or theistic and teleological evolution seems to be more appropriate than a sudden, special creation. It may even be said, in conclusion, that the Qur'anic revelation and the scientific developments in their pure essence, independent of mythological and ideological misinterpretations or misrepresentations, are not only compatible in general but also complementary and illuminatory to each other, in particular at least in the sense of encouragement and fuller explanation on the one hand, and interpretation and better understanding on the other.

DIALOGUE AND PLURALISM

The dilemma of wishing to be able to remain faithful to one's own religion and yet come to accept the validity of other traditions is one of the results of the abnormal conditions that modern men and women face and is a consequence of the anomalous conditions in which they live. Several things have happened recently to create these abnormal conditions and, looked at from a positive perspective, to shatter the attitude of religious exclusivism of the past centuries. There has been a growing awareness, generated by the media and by travel, of the sheer size and religious heterogeneity of humanity outside our own religion. 'Again, it has become evident, even to ordinary people, that in the great majority of cases the religion in which a person believes and to which he adheres depends on where he was born.... Another factor making for change is that the old unflattering caricatures of other religions are now being replaced by knowledge based on serious objective study.' Lastly, but perhaps most importantly of all, immigration from one country to another in recent decades has brought sizeable alien religious communities to many of the world's largest cities. These recent developments have theological implications and have helped to turn the attention of the theologians of any religion to the problem of the relation of that religion to the other world religions (Hick, 1980:171–4).

Muslims today continue to experience the presence of other religions in their midst as they have done over the centuries. By and large, through most periods of Islamic history, the relations between Muslims and religious minorities living in their midst have been peaceful. On the intellectual plane, there is a great deal of interest in religious dialogue in the Islamic world today. There have been some exclusivists who have opposed such dialogues, but the activity of religious dialogue has gone on for decades in the Islamic world and is now an important part of the current Islamic religious and intellectual landscape.

There are various types and aims of interreligious dialogue. One of the most important is interreligious cooperation for the sake of world peace and for the good of humanity. Although this is sometimes met with misconception or misuse of the concept of dialogue by some critics, this should not be considered a reason to oppose the development of sincere and serious inter-religious dialogue and cooperation. For the world really needs peace and there certainly are great possibilities for religions to contribute, especially if they cooperate with each other.

If religions would really like to contribute to world peace, first of all they must attain a better situation of peace and amity among themselves. In order to reach this higher position, they must lay emphasis on their common ground or similar points in oral and written encounters rather than on their differences and the points that separate them; the latter have been empha-sised for years and have often caused useless polemics and feelings of exclu-siveness and hostility. Compared to the traditional paradigm and style of past relationships, this new era of history must seek those concepts that are most similar and held in common and these must be given precedence for the sake of dialogue and cooperation.

For example, if a concept or value were shared by and respected among all the major religions, then it would really be an appropriate and impor-tant starting point for the development of a constructive dialogue. Moreover, if this concept or value were common to and respected by philosophy and science, as well as among the religions, then it would be much more signifi-cant. For this would mean that this concept or value is really one of those global concepts and values that are rarely found. Furthermore, if this concept or value were also a dialogic and peaceful one, then it would be priceless as a means of establishing not only an interreligious but also an interdisciplinary dialogue for the sake of world peace.

One of the main concepts associated with interreligious dialogue is reli-gious pluralism. John Hick is the main representative of modern religious pluralism. His pluralism has both theological and philosophical dimensions. In his earlier and more theological writings, he suggested a Copernican revo-lution in the theology of religions. The 'needed Copernican revolution in theology', according to Hick, 'involves a shift from the dogma that Chris-tianity is at the centre to the realization that it is *God* who is at the centre, and that all the religions of mankind, including our own, serve and revolve around him' (Hick 1988:131). In his later and more philosophical writings, he presents religious pluralism as a particular theory, which is philosophically dependent mainly on some Kantian ideas. Based on the Kantian distinction between noumenon and phenomenon, or between the Real *an sich* and the Real as variously thought and experienced by individuals, Hick argues that, in the particular case of religious awareness, there appear to be two basic concepts through which the Real is humanly thought and experienced, the Real as personal and the Real as nonpersonal.

For Hick, 'we never experience the Real *an sich* but always as it is finitely, inadequately, and no doubt often distortedly thought of and per-ceived by different human communities of faith…. Like the ancient parable of the elephant and the blind men…so it is with the different religions:

each identifies the Real in terms of its own partial experience of it' (Hick, 1987:333). So the religions are equal in the fact that none of them knows the real properly; and so there cannot be any superiority among them. They are also equal to be 'a range of human responses to a transcendent divine reality' (ibid.). There cannot be ethical criteria to compare and contrast the religions, either. Therefore, all the great world religions are equal among themselves; for none of them knows the Real properly, all of them are human responses and all of them transform human existence from self-centredness to reality-centredness.

Before entering the issue of religious pluralism, we should mention our ideas about exclusivism and inclusivism in a few sentences. Although exclusivism may be natural and normal for devout people who were brought up in an exclusivist environment and education, or for some people who were in a self-defensive position in relation to religion, it may be argued that it is one of the excesses of the Middle Ages and modernity. For it is an obvious fact that basic religious, spiritual and ethical truths and values do not belong to only one religion, and that other religions are not completely devoid of them. Since God has attributes such as mercy, justice and wisdom, God will pay to everybody what he or she deserves exactly and justly in the hereafter. Moreover, it is known that families usually play an important role in belonging to a religion, and it is not easy to change a religion or to convert to another one psychologically and sociologically. Although it usually stems from a strong belief and a sincere religiosity, when it is thought empathetically, one can understand that absolute religious exclusivism cannot easily be defended even in religious terms. In this case, almost no kind of exclusivism, including religious forms, should be left.

Inclusivism is a positive development in the right direction. Looked at from a religious point of view, it does not require religious people to make too many radical changes in the theological conceptions of their own religion and other religions. Although it is unacceptable for one religion to be seen as the sole source of religious truth and salvation, it does not diminish the believers' belief and trust in and their love of their own religion. However, it seems that inclusivism is a narrower or less common concept than exclusivism and pluralism. Moreover, Christian inclusivists' ideas about seeing the members of other religions as anonymous Christians and their view of other religions as a preparation to Christianity are too particularistic and anachronistic. The historical period in which one religion was seen as a preparation for another is long past.

Some Muslim approaches to other religions, which may perhaps be called Islamic inclusivism, also seem encouraging but do not go far enough. For they seem to widen the circle of religiously considerable truth and salvation to cover the three Abrahamic religions, in other words, the People of the Book, but apparently no further (see, for example, Ates, 1999–2000). This is positive, but there are also millions of sincerely religious people worshipping God and praying in the most general sense of the word and doing good deeds for the purpose of salvation, again in a general sense, outside these three Abrahamic faiths. Is it fair and plausible to overlook them? Therefore, it seems better to go beyond inclusivism, too, and to try to solve the problem of religious plurality and religious peace under the terms of religious pluralism.

Even if religious pluralism has become more widespread in intellectual environments in recent decades, as even Hick himself sometimes points out, it has not yet occupied a central position among religious people. Why is this so? Is it a structural problem or not? It seems to us that the popular Hickian religious pluralism has some philosophical, particularly Kantian, dimensions that may seem too radical to some people and may therefore cause it to remain marginal. However, such a dimension is neither necessary nor useful for a properly or sufficiently religious version of religious pluralism. It may, at this stage, be useful to make some criticisms and suggestions to promote a non-radical and more moderate and religious version of religious pluralism. While this concept of religious pluralism should submit to the right of other religions to promise truth and salvation, it should not shake or weaken the believers' faith and trust in their own religion, either. We can enumerate some of our tentative proposals for a non-radical pluralism.

First, it seems to us that, while Hick's Copernican God-centred revolution in theology is perfectly all right, his Kantian distinction between the Real *an sich* and the Real as variously thought and experienced by individuals, and his assertion based on this distinction that this type of dualistic concept of God as personal and non-personal can be found in every religion are neither necessary and useful for a theory of religious pluralism nor easily acceptable for the believers of the monotheistic religions. The main theological emphasis of Islam, for example, is the oneness and uniqueness of God; and even an implicit dualism is quite alien to Islam and does not sound well to the ear of any ordinary Muslim. Then, a non-radical pluralism should be far from any suspicion or flavour of *dualism*.

Second, Hick's Kantian emphasis that all religions' experience and knowledge of the Real are always finite, inadequate and often distorted, like the ancient parable of the elephant and the blind men shows, is again neither necessary and useful for a theory of religious pluralism nor a desirable fact to emphasis from the religious point of view. Although it is true that nobody can experience and know God, or the Real, in God's absoluteness and uniqueness, the emphasis must be on the positive side of the similarities in what the religions know or tell about God rather than on the negative side, highlighting the fact that none of them properly knows God, the Real. For this approach approximates to agnosticism, whereas religion and especially common-sense religiosity cannot live on too much agnosticism. Religiosity usually depends on believing in and trusting the truth and goodness of what the scriptures or the prophets said on their exceptional authority. Then, a non-radical pluralism should also be far from any suspicion or whiff of excessive *agnosticism*.

Third, Hick's general description of religions as 'human responses to the transcendent' also seems to be radical, in other words, to be more excessive than necessary for a religiously acceptable theory of religious pluralism. There is a belief in the transcendent here; so it is not naturalism, which sees religion as just a human projection. However, the emphasis on 'human response' in explaining the religions seems to imply that humans were the only actors in the formation of the religions and that God or the Transcendent was completely passive, probably as a non-personal reality. It associates the exclusion of the divine or transcendental factor in the religions through revelation, inspiration, providence, or some other ways. God's personal dimension and personal relation to humankind, namely, the theistic conception of God, seems to be undermined or at least underestimated from the perspective of monotheistic religions. In a famous metaphor, which Hick often quotes, the Muslim Sufi poet Rumi wrote about the different religious traditions: 'The lamps are different but the light is the same: it comes from beyond' (cited in Hick, 1987:332). The last phrase of this sentence, 'it comes from beyond', should not be neglected in any non-radical pluralism. In the simple formulation of 'human responses to the transcendent', God seems to be too pantheistic and religion seems to be too humanistic. So, a non-radical religious pluralism should not be too open to the criticism of *humanism* (in its restricted sense) and of *pantheism*.

Fourth, religions have both various world-views (belief systems, theological doctrines and teachings) and various forms of life (rituals and norms for ethical behaviour). Some of them are the same or similar among some religions and others are completely or relatively different and incompatible. It is good to emphasise the common and compatible points rather than those that are different and incompatible; but this desire does not prompt somebody to claim that a common denominator among religions, for example, the transformation of human existence from self-centredness to Real-centredness, is really important, while other theological, ritual, ethical and historical dimensions are not so important. Pluralism should not damage either the overall structure of any religion or its overall value in the eyes of its believers. It should be far from subjective and selective *reductionism*.

Fifth, non-radical pluralism should not emphasise the equality and identity of religions too much, in the way that radical exclusivism emphasised the inequality and differences among them. For both attitudes would end up abolishing people's freedom of choice among religions. If all other religions are false, as in the case of an exclusivist attitude, you do not have real freedom of choice, you must necessarily remain in your own religion as a reasonable person. And similarly, if all religions are completely equal, as may be the case of radical pluralism, again you do not have proper freedom of choice, and again, as a reasonable person, you must naturally remain in your own religion. People should not be forced to change or not to change their religion. Freedom of choice and change should always be open. A non-religious pluralism should also be far from a kind of soft or implicit *totalitarianism*.

Sixth, a more coherent and a more peaceful pluralist attitude seems to require being pluralist and tolerant of alternative theories concerning religious plurality and diversity, namely exclusivism and inclusivism. Whereas, for example, Hick can accuse exclusivism of being an 'attitude of religious imperialism' (1980:171) and Paul Knitter can accuse inclusivism as being 'open to colonialist or imperialist distortions' (cited in Coward, 2000:41), some exclusivists and inclusivists may really have shown such shortcomings, but most of them cannot have had such negative ideas and ideals. In addition, almost the same reasons for defending religious pluralism seem to be valid for believing in a pluralism of the theories of religions. All of them are equal in being an explanatory theory for religious diversity. Moreover, most of the defenders of these theories were born into a family or society that already believed that theory. So non-radical pluralism should be careful not to develop into a different kind of *exclusivism*.

These are just some of the main points that should be critically re-evaluated in a move towards non-radical pluralism. Insisting on these aspects as they are can cause religious pluralism to be seen as religiously radical and to remain marginal. However, they are not necessary from either a philosophical or religious viewpoint. From the perspective of Socratic philosophy, for example, one can believe in God and talk about God, while nonetheless being aware of the fact that the knowledge arrived at is very limited. Philo–sophia means the love of and search for wisdom in spite of the fact that one will never arrive at the real wisdom. In addition to this, Socrates talks about how God inspired him to make decisions. For him, his thoughts and beliefs are not only his human responses to the transcendent; the transcendent inspires him, too. Philosophically, Karl Popper can also supply inspiration for or insight into a non-radical religious pluralism. He defends a critical pluralism against a relativistic one, which, according to him, places society under the hegemony of violence. The thought of truth, or rather the search for truth occupies a very considerable place in his critical pluralism. These philosophical ideas, too, seem illuminating for a non-radical religious pluralism.

Looked at from the religious, and particularly Islamic, point of view, one can see the divine factor not only in one religion, as in the case of exclusivism, or in the three Abrahamic religions, as in the case of inclusivism, but also in all the great or genuine religions of the world. For the Qur'an clearly states that '... there never was a people, without a warner having lived among them (in the past)' (35:24). It also points out what the essence or common core of their message was: 'For We assuredly sent amongst every People a Messenger (with the command), "Serve Allah, and eschew Evil"...' (16:36). Since all the great religions have these two basic essences, even if in a general sense and to different degrees, they have a common core and value on a positive basis (rather than a negative equality of not knowing the Real *an sich*). Similarly, the Qur'an also mentions three basic essences shared particularly among the Abrahamic religions; and it adds that all believers will have what they justly deserve in the hereafter: 'Those who believe (in the Qur'an), and those who follow the Jewish (scriptures), and the Christians and the Sabians, any who believe in Allah and the Last Day, and work righteousness, shall have their reward with their Lord on them shall be no fear, nor shall they grieve' (2:62). Therefore, a non-radical religious pluralism can depend on common positive values among the religions rather than on ideas associating philosophical dualism and agnosticism.

Moreover, for a non-radical religious pluralism, the divine factor should also be recognised, together with human factors, both in the formation and in the differentiation of religions. This factor increases the believer's respect of other religions as well as his or her own religion. Indeed, the Qur'an mentions both the divine factor in the diversity of religions and the ideal attitude of religious people in the face of the reality of religious plurality: '... To each among you have We prescribed a Law and an Open Way. If Allah had so willed, He would have made you a single People, but (His Plan is) to test you in what He hath given you: so strive as in a race in all virtues. The goal of you all is to Allah; it is He that will show you the truth of the matters in which ye dispute' (5:48). This verse may be considered to summarise the theoretical essence and practical principles of a religiously non-radical version of religious pluralism.

Muslims should not make a similar mistake on this issue, as, according to the Qur'an, Jews and Christians had made before. The adherents of each of these two religions had claimed that only they would go to Paradise, as the Qur'an points out: 'And they say: "None shall enter Paradise unless he be a Jew or a Christian." Those are their (vain) desires. Say: "Produce your proof if ye are truthful"' (2:111). Now some Muslims have asserted similar exclusivist or monopolist views concerning Paradise. The Qur'anic principle in the following verses , however, is very clear and obvious: 'Not your desires, nor those of the People of the Book (can prevail): whoever works evil, will be requited accordingly. Nor will he find, besides Allah, any protector or helper. If any do deeds of righteousness, – be they male or female – and have faith, they will enter Heaven, and not the least injustice will be done to them' (4:123–4).

The Qur'an does not condemn outright the adherents of any religion to Hell, and instead affirms that there are good people and bad people among every religious community, and the good ones will enter Paradise. For example, the Qur'an says about Jews that 'there is from among them a party of the right course: But many of them follow a course that is evil' (5:66). These verses show the general laws of Allah, the divine principle on this issue:

Not all of them are alike: Of the People of the Book are a portion that stand (for the right); they rehearse the Signs of Allah all night long, and they prostrate themselves in adoration. They believe in Allah, and the Last Day; they enjoin what is right, and forbid what is wrong; and they hasten (in emulation) in (all) good works: They are in the ranks of the righteous. Of the good that they do, nothing will be rejected of them; for Allah knoweth well those that do right. (3:113–15)

Also, the Qur'an does not state that every Muslim who says he or she believes in Muhammad the Last Prophet will enter Paradise. For faith does not consist of their word alone. The Qur'an gives numerous attributes of the Muslim believers who will enter the paradise, as in this verse): 'Those who patiently persevere, seeking the countenance of their Lord; establish regular prayers; spend, out of (the gifts) We have bestowed for their sustenance, secretly and openly; and turn of evil with good: for such there is the final attainment of the (eternal) Home' (13:22).

Therefore, we can say that, while we try to escape from the religious exclusivism of modernity with its one-sided excessiveness, we should not be caught in the radical religious pluralism of postmodernity with its relativistic and agnostic excessiveness. Religious pluralism should be a non-radical theory, particularly from a religious point of view, so that it does not remain a marginal intellectual movement among some philosophers of religion and liberal theologians. In addition, after modernity, we should also pass from the phase of theoretical discussions about religious pluralism to a higher phase with a practical or 'sophialogical' dimension to call the world together to 'eschew evil', all forms of violence and war, as well as injustices and immoralities, and to 'strive as in a race in all virtues' and values together.

TERROR AND PEACE

It is not easy to define terrorism and determine its difference from murder, guerrilla warfare, armed resistance and war – and *jihad* in an Islamic context. However, it is important to define it as a whole and to differentiate its specific methods in order to analyse it properly and to evaluate it from the perspective of genuine religious and Islamic values. Terrorism can be defined as 'a strategy, a method by which an organized group or party tries to get attention for its aims, or force concessions toward its goals, through the systematic use of deliberate violence. Typical terrorists are individuals trained and disciplined to carry out the violence decided upon by their organizations' (Watson, 1976:1). Among the leanest and most effective definitions upon which nearly all might agree is the *intentional* targeting of civilians, including women and children, for political ends.

Terrorism is a complex problem. Its origins are diverse, and those who engage in it, even more so. Any attempt to understand the motivations and actions of terrorist individuals and groups must obviously take into account that enormous diversity. At the extreme, what makes a man or woman become a terrorist? A variety of complex impulses come into play – with material, social, cultural and psychological foundations all affecting individual human behaviour. Some of the possible factors behind the violent terrorist acts may include hatred and prejudice, fear and powerlessness, occupation and domination, injustice and suffering, corruption and greed, oppression and control, dictatorship and total authority, debt, poverty and hunger, frustration and helplessness, and dislike of inclusive society (Sajid, 2001:18).

A most arresting and unexpected development in recent years has been the revival of terrorist activities to support religious purposes or terror justified in theological terms, a phenomenon that, according to some writers, might be called 'holy' or 'sacred' terror.

Today terror has been globalised in one sense, and almost nowhere in the world is very far from actual or potential terrorism of any sort, religionist, secularist or nationalist. This loads great responsibility on the intellectuals and religious scholars as well as on politicians and others. Everyone should do his or her best against any kind of terrorism, or better still, against any kind of violence. It must be argued that no sort of terror or violence against innocent civilians can be a legal, reasonable, and admissible instrument for any noble purpose whatsoever from the perspective of any religion, ideology or nation. It is not right to arrive at a good aim through a bad instrument; the nobility of the aim does not make an illegal, brutal instrument legal and noble. Violence produces more violence; and more violence prevents or at least delays the spiritual evolution of individuals, including our own religious or national fellow brothers, sisters for generations to come.

From a Muslim perspective, it is good, first of all, to hear the truth from some non-Muslim writers that Islam is not 'intrinsically linked to terrorism – it is probably not so linked any more than are, say, Christianity, Judaism, and Hinduism, within each of which, at some point, terrorist movements have arisen' (Reich, 1990:3). There is plenty of evidence of fantasy throughout the history of anti-Islamic stereotypes. As a non-Muslim author righteously writes, 'Muslims are considered to be violent, yet we do not hear any similar accusations about intrinsic violence in Christianity or European culture; what was it about Christianity that motivated the world conquests of the nineteenth century or more recent atrocities such as the 1996 massacre of more than 6,000 Muslim men and boys carried out in a single day by Eastern Orthodox Serbs in Srebrenica?' (Ernst, 2003:28).

Islam seeks to attain a world of peace and justice. 'But just as Christianity, Judaism, Hinduism, Shintoism, and other religions have been used by radicals to justify violent and ugly actions, so too has Islam. Monotheistic faiths in particular offer a few scriptural passages, drawn out of ancient and specific historical context, that call for graphic and terrible acts in God's name against the enemies of the true faith' (Fuller, 2003: 88). For instance, one can find verses from the Qur'an proclaiming war against the pagan Arabs of Mecca, who were engaged in a bitter struggle against Muhammad. These have been used as evidence that Muslims are perennially engaged in warfare against all non-Muslims. Yet few would accept the similar passages that can easily be found in the Hebrew Bible (Deut. 32:41–2) or in the New Testament (Matt. 10:34). While there may be fundamentalists who insist on the unlimited applicability of every verse of this type, most Jews, Christians and Muslims would assert that such sayings reflect particular historical situations and are limited to those contexts. They would further argue that there are overriding moral and peaceful themes and principles in the holy books that take precedence over individual verses.

Most Muslims are strongly opposed to acts of violence, in any form, undertaken in the name of religion. Consequently, it hurts them to constantly see the name of Islam, 'the religion of peace', linked with international terrorism. While all Muslims point out that Islam is basically a religion of peace, the violence of a tiny handful of extreme radicals was able to dominate the perception of Islam by others in much of the world.

Terrorism, which invariably makes indiscriminate use of force causing destruction of civilian life and property, including women, children and old people, is a crime against humanity under Islam as much as under humanitarian law. Islam is a religion of peace and moderation. The Qur'an defines Muslims as the well-balanced middle nation, a model for the others (2:143) and advised them not to follow extremism in religious interpretation (4:171, 5:77, and 22:78). Islam and terrorism are contradictory terms opposed to each other. Islam condemns and rejects all forms of terror, killing without due process of law. There is no justification for the use of terms such as 'Islamic terrorists'. Islam upholds sanctity of human life as paramount, and the Qur'an declares that killing one innocent human being is like killing the entire human race (5:32, 6:151, and 17:33):

> Whosoever kills a human being for other than manslaughter or corruption in the earth, it shall be as if he had killed all mankind, and whoso saves the life of the one, it shall be as if he had saved the life of all mankind. (5:32)

The issue for Muslims is complicated when the use of the term *jihad* is invoked in Islamist politics or adopted by terrorists. The basic meaning of jihad is 'to struggle'. In Islam the 'greater jihad' is the struggle of the individual to overcome one's own baser instincts; 'lesser jihad' is the use of force to *defend* one's family or the community from any attacks. The Qur'an says that 'Fight for the sake of Allah those that who fight against you, but do not attack them first. Allah does not love the aggressors' (2:190). It is also pointed out in the Qur'an that 'Allah only forbids you to make friends with those who have fought against you on account of your religion and driven you from your homes, or abetted others to do so' (60:9). The fact that war is only permitted to defend basic human rights, such as the right to live and the right to worship freely, is also explained in this verse:

> (Fighting is) permitted to those who are fought against, because they were wronged; and surely Allah is Able to help them. Those who have been expelled unjustly from their homes only for the reason that they said: 'Our Lord is Allah'. For had it not been for Allah's repelling some men by means of others, monasteries, churches, synagogues, and mosques, wherein the name of Allah is often mentioned, would have been demolished. (Qur'an, 22:39–40)

Briefly speaking, in Islam, just as an end must be legitimate, so must all the means employed to reach that end. From this perspective, one cannot achieve Heaven by murdering another person. Peace is essential and war is the last resort in Islam; and war is subject to the rigorous conditions laid down by the law, which include prohibitions against harming civilians. It makes a distinction between belligerents and combatants; it does not permit the killing of minors, women, the very old, the sick and monks; debts in favour of the citizens of the enemy country are not touched by the declaration of war; all killing or devastation beyond the strict indispensable minimum is forbidden; prisoners are well treated and their acts of belligerency are not considered as crimes. As the most general principle, the Qur'an says that 'if they incline to peace, incline also to it, and trust in Allah' (8:61). It has many other verses of tolerance and peace. It is said, for example, that 'Good and evil deeds are not equal. Repel evil with what is better; you will see that he with whom you had enmity has become your dearest friend' (41:34). Therefore, the basic principle of Islam, of which the original name means peace, really is and always should be search for the ground of dialogue, reconciliation and living together in a common core of justice and peace.

HUMAN RIGHTS AND DEMOCRACY

Although the term 'human rights' has only recently come into common use, two more comprehensive concepts concerning rights have always existed in the Muslim world: the rights of God (*haqooqullah*) and the rights of God's creatures (*haqooqulabad*), including men, women, children, non-Muslims, animals, plants and physical objects. Islam divides crimes into two main categories: those that are committed against the rights of God (unbelief, neglect of worship, etc.), and those against the rights of God's creatures, especially human beings. Moreover, God does not pardon the harm done by a man to his fellow being: it is the victim who alone can pardon. If one does harm to another creature, be it man, animal or any other living being, one commits in fact a double crime: a crime against one's immediate victim, and also a crime against God, since the criminal conduct in question constitutes a violation of the divine prescriptions. Thus, it is possible to say that human rights is a subcategory of the more comprehensive and classical category of every creature's rights in Islam.

In his celebrated speech, on the occasion of the Farewell Pilgrimage, the Prophet declared the inviolability of the rights of a man in all the three categories of person, property and honour. He said that 'Your lives and properties are forbidden to one another till you meet your Lord on the day of Resurrection.' The right to life is the most essential one guaranteed for every individual. Even during a state of war, protection is guaranteed for those who ask for it, even if he or she is a polytheist: 'If any polytheist seeks your protection,' the Qur'an says, 'then protect him so that he may hear the word of Allah, then convey him to a place where he can be secure' (9:6). The Qur'an upholds the sanctity and absolute value of human life, saying that 'you slay not the life which Allah has made sacred' (6:151) and points out that, in essence, the life of each individual is comparable to that of an entire community and, therefore, should be treated with the utmost care: 'whosoever kills a human being for other than manslaughter or corruption in the earth, it shall be as if he had killed all mankind, and whosoever saves the life of one, it shall be as if he had saved the life of all mankind' (5:32).

Nevertheless, the modern concept of human rights lacks precise equivalents in Islamic doctrines, and in the nineteenth and especially the latter half of the twentieth century, the question of the compatibility of international human rights principles with Islamic doctrine was raised. It was in the aftermath of World War II that the modern international formulations of human rights were produced. Muslim countries were among the founding members of the United Nations, whose 1945 Charter called for respect for human rights and fundamental freedoms. By the end of the twentieth century all Muslim countries had adopted constitutions containing some or all of the rights principles set forth in international human rights law. Governments and individuals throughout the Muslim world continue to take many positive positions on human rights.

Freedom of religion and conscience is laid down by the Qur'an itself: 'Let there be no compulsion in religion' (2:256). This means that, according to Qur'anic teaching, non-Muslims living in Muslim territories should have the freedom to follow their own faith-traditions without fear or harassment. A number of Qur'anic passages state clearly that the responsibility of the Prophet Muhammad is to communicate the message of God and not to compel anyone to believe (see 6:107; 10:99; 16:82; 42:48). History provides many examples of Muslims' respect towards other faiths. A well-known example is when Omar, the second successor to Prophet Muhammad, entered Jerusalem. He refused to pray inside the Church of the Holy Sepulchre. He was concerned that some overzealous Muslim in the future might destroy the Church and build a Mosque in his honour.

Although it is controversial to some extent, the freedom of religion is guaranteed not only for non-Muslims but also for Muslims. That is to say, 'the freedom to convert to another faith after accepting Islam is left to man's essential free choice'. If freedom of belief is guaranteed and secured against enforcement, in accordance with the verse saying 'no compulsion in religion', the Muslim-born individual's right to change his or her religion is also protected. The result of an individual's choice will be seen in the life after death. Although some penalties were later introduced by jurists and institutionalised as part of the faith, 'there is no immediate worldly penalty mentioned for such an act in the Qur'an' (Zayd, 2004:6; Hassan, 2006). Two verses may be quoted from the Qur'an in this context: 'Say: "(*It is*) the Truth from your Lord". Now whosoever will, may believe, and whosoever will, may disbelieve. For the wrong-doers We have prepared a fire...' (18:29; see also 3:90 and 4:137). 'O you who believe! If any from among you turn back from his religion, Allah will bring a people whom He loves and who love Him ...' (5:54).

When it comes to human equality, it is obvious, at least in theory, that racism and sexual discrimination are incomprehensible to Muslims; for the Qur'an speaks of human equality in the following terms: 'O mankind! We created you from a single (pair) of a male and a female, and made you into nations and tribes, that ye may know each other (not that ye may despise each other). Verily the most honoured of you in the sight of Allah is (he who is) the most righteous of you' (49:13).

In this verse, God makes it clear that the only criterion for superiority amongst peoples is piety and righteousness. Nowhere does the Qur'an state that one gender or one nation is superior to another. Although in some Muslim countries and societies a patriarchal culture is dominant and women are sometimes denied their rights, Islam recognises women as individuals with specific rights, such as the right to life, the right to learn, the right to earn, own and dispose property, the right to choose her husband, the right to retain her maiden name, the right to be treated equally, the right to seek divorce and the right to inherit. Women and men are also equally rewarded in the hereafter for a righteously led life, according to the Qur'an: '... those that have faith and do good works, whether male or female, shall enter the Garden' (40:40).

When we look at the authoritative Islamic scriptures, we can see prominent resources for an ethic of gender equality. Even gender-specific language had clearly become a concern in the early Muslim community. A number of women approached the Prophet to ask him about the prevalence of male pronouns in the Qur'an, wanting to know if women were included in these statements. The next revelations of the Qur'an responded directly to these concerns, with balanced phrases that make it clear that men and women share equally in the religious life:

Behold; men who surrender to Allah, and women who surrender, and men who believe and women who believe, and men who obey and women who obey, and men who speak the truth and women who speak the truth, and men who persevere (in righteousness) and women who persevere, and men who are humble and women who are humble, and men who give alms and women who give alms, and men who fast and women who fast, and men who guard their modesty and women who guard (*their modesty*), and men who remember Allah much and women who remember, Allah has prepared for them forgiveness and a vast reward. (33:35)

Women have never been ciphers or nonentities, even in early Muslim society. The wives of the Prophet Muhammad were his partners and supporters in the creation of the new society, and they continued to have eminence after his death. The position of women as mothers is very exalted in Islamic tradition. The Prophet Muhammad went so far as to say: 'Even Paradise lies underneath the feet of your mothers.' As regards the woman as wife, the saying of the Prophet is well known: 'The best among you is the one who is best towards his wife.' Muslim women engaged in every profession that suited them, not only as mother, wife, sister or daughter. They worked as nurses, teachers and even as combatants by the side of men when necessary, as well as being singers and hairdressers. Caliph 'Umar employed a lady, Shifa' bint 'Abdallah, as an inspector in the market at Medina. The same lady had taught Hafsah, wife of the Prophet, how to write and read. There are several examples of this kind.

Islamic law in theory also provides resources for women, such as property rights, which were not available to many women until very recent times. 'Yet, in practice, the complex application of Islamic law was filtered through multiple levels of custom and tradition, so that ethical principles of equality between the sexes all too frequently were sacrificed for the benefit of male privilege. However, the imposition of patriarchal authority over women is hardly unique to Islamic civilisation....Disentangling the roles of the ethics of gender and patriarchal history is a task that now is being undertaken in every culture, even when it does not bear the name of feminism' (Ernst, 2003:142–5; Hamidullah, 1980:184–9). Where women have virtually no rights, as in certain tribal areas, it should be attributed to local traditions and historical conditions not to Islamic advice, and it is of course a matter in need of urgent redress.

Together with the concept of human rights, in recent decades many Muslims have also accepted the notion of democracy but differed as to its precise meaning. The Islamisation of democracy has been based on a modern reinterpretation of traditional Islamic concepts of political deliberation or consultation (*shura*), community consensus (*ijma*), public interests (*al-maslahah*), justice (*'adl*), no compulsion in religion (*la ikraha fi al-din*), and personal interpretation (*ijtihad*) or reinterpretation to support notions of parliamentary democracy, representative elections, and the equality of citizens in civic rights and duties. There may be some differences between Western notions of democracy and Islamic traditions. However, 'increased emphasis on political liberalization, electoral politics, and democratization does not necessarily imply uncritical acceptance of Western forms of democracy. ....Islam possesses or can generate its own distinctive forms of democracy' (Esposito, 1992:186–7). In this respect, the Qur'an does not prescribe hard and fast methods. The number, the form of election, the duration of representation are left to the discretion of the leaders of every age and every country. The aim of all representation is that the government should always remain in touch with public opinion.

> The [contemporary] Muslim world needs to institute and ensure the success of democracy. While the practice of democracy in the Muslim world has been disappointing and is synonymous with corruption and mismanagement, in the end there is no alternative. It is the only system that allows corrupt leaders to be removed with minimal friction....Muslims must be able to feel that they can participate in the process of governance. They must feel that they are able to elect their leaders and that if those leaders are not able to deliver, that they can throw them out as well....With a working democracy Muslims will be able to ensure that the gaps that are widening between the rich and the poor will be bridged. (Ahmed, 2003:153–4)

The redistribution of wealth and the proper establishment of human rights, freedom and dignity must remain major priorities of any democratic government.

Animal rights in Islam may also be mentioned in a few sentences from Hamidullah.

> In a famous saying of his, the Prophet Muhammad gave a warning, that on Doomsday, a certain person would be thrown in Hell because he had tied up a cat with a rope, giving it neither to eat nor to drink, nor letting it go and seek itself the food, thus causing the poor animal's death through inanition. In another Hadith, the Prophet spoke of divine punishment to those men who did not fulfil their duty even to animals by not giving them sufficient food, or loading them beyond their strength. The Prophet prohibited even the hewing down of trees if it was not necessary. (Hamidullah, 1980:120)

POSTMODERNISM AND THE FUTURE

Modernity is commonly defined in terms of the values of the European Enlightenment of the seventeenth and eighteenth centuries. The great seventeenth-century thinker Descartes is usually seen as the founder of philosophical modernism and as the first modern philosopher. One of the basic characteristics of Descartes' philosophy in particular and of modernity in general was its strictly foundationalist, rationalist, objectivist, universalist and particularly dualist structure in epistemology and in other intellectual perspectives, as well as ontology. Thus, modernism has come to mean the recent phase of world history marked by belief in rationality, science, planning, progress and secularism. The modernist tendency defined religion as a system of personal belief rather than as a way of life. Its restricted definition has become accepted as the norm or meaning of religion by many believers and unbelievers alike in the West.

The Muslim modernist phase was engendered by European colonialism. While more conservative Muslims would have no truck with Europeans, the modernists wished to come to terms with and even incorporate elements of their civilisation. Most sought synthesis and ideally looked for harmony between their own position and that of the Europeans.

More secularist modernists blamed an outmoded tradition. They advocated the separation of religion and politics, and the establishment of modern nation states modelled on the West. For them Islam should be restricted to personal life and public life should be modelled on modern, that is, European ideas. They adopted Western manners, dress, music and movies, and appropriated Europe's political, economic, educational and legal institutions.

More Islamic modernists or reform-minded Muslims sought to delineate an alternative to Western, secular adaptationism on the one hand and religiously motivated rejectionism of modernity on the other. They blamed the internal decline of Muslim societies, their loss of power and backwardness, and their inability to respond effectively to European colonialism on a blind and unquestioned clinging to the past (*taqlid*). On the contrary, they stressed the dynamism, flexibility and adaptability that had characterised the early development of Islam. They pressed for internal reform through a process of reinterpretation (*ijtihad*) and selective adaptation of Western ideas.

Islamic modernism was a process of internal self-criticism, a struggle to redefine Islam to demonstrate its relevance to the new situations that Muslims found themselves in as their societies modernised. While their secular counterparts looked to the West rather uncritically and traditionalists shunned the West rather obstinately, Islamic modernists attempted to establish a continuity between their Islamic heritage and modern change. However, both secularist and Islamic modernists failed to produce an integrated, new synthesis or interpretation of Islam. Their isolated, ad hoc reforms were not seen as part of an integrated whole, but instead as the result of an eclectic borrowing from the West. Therefore, modernists usually came to be regarded as Westernisers (Esposito, 1991:125–54).

As its name suggests, postmodernism defines itself in opposition to modernism or modernity. Various influences have contributed over the last forty years to the making of postmodernism. When the values of modernity had almost won the war and established hegemony over its alternatives, modernism failed to achieve the worldly paradise it had promised, and it started to be criticised. The other values and perspectives which modernity had fought, denied or neglected then began to flourish and spread out. The new postmodern values reflected the reaction to the extreme one-sidedness of modernity and the postmodernists have defended the other edge as strictly as their predecessors did. Instead of the dualist rhetoric of fighting for the one against the others, postmodernists have defended a relativist and pluralist perspective towards the alternative epistemological or cultural differences and diversities. For them, there are no certain boundaries between truth and falsehood, objectivity and subjectivity, good or bad; and there are no objective criteria to decide what is right and what is wrong, except personal and pragmatic preferences. Everything is historical, cultural and subjective; and thus every thought, belief or behaviour is relative, legitimate and equally valid. There is no real superiority among the alternatives or diversities. All the differences must be seen from the perspective of richness, creativity, tolerance and equality.

Essentially concerned with ambiguity, the term 'postmodernism' is difficult to define unambiguously. It is usually characterised as an 'incredulity toward metanarratives', a questioning of the project of modernity, a heightened scepticism of traditional faiths, and finally 'a rejection of a view of the world as a universal totality, of the expectation of final solutions and complete answers'. 'In order to discover postmodernism one must look for richness of meaning rather than clarity of meaning; avoid choices between black and white, "either–or" and accept "both–and"; evoke many levels of meaning and combinations of focus; and attempt self-discovery through self-knowledge.' Postmodernism allows the 'juxtaposition of discourses, an exuberant eclecticism, the mixing of diverse images. The postmodernist montage mixes the highbrow and the populist, the alienating and the accessible; the taste is eclectic....The eclecticism feeds from the diverse and unexpected bringing together of widely different discourses' (Ahmed, 1992:10, 25).

Briefly speaking, among the views that go under the rubric of postmodernism are to be found 'a rejection of classical foundationalism; the claim that there is no such thing as objectivity; the claim that there is no such thing as truth, or that if there is, it is something totally different from what we thought; the claim that truths are made, not discovered; the claim that there are no objective normative standards; the claim that all that really matters is power. There is the insistence that God is dead. There is historicism, the idea that our historical and cultural setting determines what we can think', and also 'celebration of diversity' (Plantinga, 2000:422–4).

Looked at from the religious point of view, one can say together with Alvin Plantinga that some of them are entirely congenial to religion like the rejection of classical foundationalism or the sympathy and compassion for the poor and oppressed; some other postmodern claims, however, do appear to be incompatible with religious belief: 'for example, the claims that God is dead, that there are no 'objective' moral standards, and perhaps also the claim that there isn't any such thing as truth, at least as commensensically thought of' (ibid.:423–4).

In a similar way, while Muslims appreciate the rejection of modernism, the importance of diversity, the spirit of tolerance, the necessity for under-standing the other, concern for the less privileged, optimism and the drive for self-knowledge in postmodernism, 'they also recognise the threat it poses them with its cynicism and irony. This is a challenge to the faith and piety which lies at the core of their world-view' (Ahmed, 1992:6).

In fact, both the modernist concept of absolutism and the postmodern-ist concept of relativism have bright and shadow sides. The virtue of the absolute is the power it offers the soul; its danger is the fanaticism into which the power can narrow. In the case of postmodern relativism, its main virtue is tolerance and nihilism is its shadow side (Smith, 1996:501). Because it is understood that postmodernism has both positive and negative sides, in relation to culture in general and religion in particular, it should neither be accepted nor be rejected in total.

It also seems that it would be better to interpret it in a positive manner, looking at its 'positive sides, like diversity, the freedom to explore, the break-down of establishment structures and the possibility to know and understand one another. Postmodernism need not be viewed as an intellectual conceit, an academic discussion remote from actual life in literary salons, but as an historic phase of human history offering possibilities not available before to such large numbers; a phase that holds the possibility of bringing diverse people and cultures closer together than ever before.' Postmodernism, with its emphasis on plurality, equality and tolerance, will perhaps encourage friend-ships and cooperation amongst human beings (Ahmed, 1992:27, 191).

It seems possible to look at the relationship between modernity and postmodernity from the historical relationship between Islamic dogmatic theology (*kalam*) and Islamic mysticism (Sufism). For a while they and their representatives were friendly to each other in the golden age of Islamic history, but in later centuries the former have emphasised almost exclusively such concepts as reason, science, evidence, truth, exclusivistic criteria for salvation, responsibility, justice and so on, and the latter have laid stress upon heart, gnosis, experience, love, forgiveness, tolerance, diversity in unity, liberty and mercy. It is quite obvious that the concepts advocated by theologians were similar to the ones advocated by modernists; and that the values defended by Sufis were also similar to the values defended now by the postmodernists. Just as some Muslims today advocate a modernist Islamic theology, rejecting Sufism as an external innovation, they may advocate modernism rejecting postmodernism. And just as some Sufis defend mystical Islam, criticising Islamic theology as too dogmatic and dry, they may be pleased to welcome postmodernism criticising modernism.

However, if a Muslim sees Islamic theology and mysticism as mutually supporting and complementary to each other in their moderate versions rather than as mutually excluding and conflicting, he or she can also see modernity and postmodernity in a similar way. It seems that such an approach is better both for the relation of theology and mysticism and of modernity and postmodernity, provided that they are represented in their moderate interpretations, not in extreme and exclusive positions. For a religion like Islam can neither be happy with an extremely modern definition of religion as just a theoretical system of personal belief in individual's mind, nor be pleased with an extremely postmodern description of religion, such as 'belonging without believing', or 'religion without religion/God'. But, on the contrary, it is completely compatible both with moderately interpreted modern ideas, such as rationality, objectivity, unity and truth, and with moderately understood postmodern values, such as spirituality, subjectivity, plurality and equality.

Modernity and postmodernity as well as rational theology and Sufi spirituality actually complement each other; and for a religion like Islam, theological or modern concepts usually come first, and mystical or postmodern concepts follow and complement them. This does not mean that they should be combined together with all their historical innovations, excesses and hardships. All the traditional sciences and schools should be understood in accordance with the main source, the Qur'an, and all the excess baggage loaded on the shoulders of Muslims during the history should be jettisoned carefully. It should be known that rapid change is a reality in contemporary world, including the Islamic world and Muslim societies. It should be allowed that change and development in the right direction occurs in stability by evolutionary processes. The true understanding of the Qur'an and Islamic sciences, and the proper appreciation of postmodern process and change, is essential and critical in the coming years not only for Muslims but also for the whole of humanity who have to live together on a small globe in peace and harmony.

It seems also possible to look at modernity and postmodernity from the perspective of the historical relationship between Islamic concepts of knowledge ('ilm) and wisdom (hikmah). Both knowledge and wisdom have many definitions and it is difficult to give a commonly accepted definition for them. Generally speaking, while knowledge is an intellectual product of the mental activity of individuals mainly concerning the true description of the related objects or states of affairs, wisdom is an intellectual, emotional, volitional and spiritual characteristics of some people in relation not only to the true knowledge of the objects but also to the true knowledge of the self, and to valuable words and virtuous actions. It is understood, therefore, that although they are closely related to each other, while knowledge is more theoretical and intellectual, wisdom is more practical and experiential.

When looking at the relationship between knowledge and wisdom from the historical perspective, it can be seen that they are accompanying concepts, in a complementary and productive dialogue. There are numerous verses in the Bible and the Qur'an on the subject of knowledge and wisdom, and some of them are stated together. The following are just a few examples among many: 'To the man who pleases him, God gives wisdom, knowledge and happiness' (Eccles. 2:26); 'Christ, in whom are hidden all the treasures of wisdom and knowledge' (Col. :2–3); '… We gave him (Joseph) wisdom and knowledge, thus We reward the doers of good …' (Qur'an 12:22). These examples show that knowledge and wisdom are neither identical nor unconnected concepts. They emphasise and encourage both the relationship between each other and their relationship with virtue, happiness and eschatological reward.

According to a widespread conviction among Muslims, there have been many expositions on the nature of knowledge in Islam, more than in any other religion, culture and civilisation, and this is due to the preeminent position and paramount role accorded to *al-'ilm* by God in the Holy Qur'an. Islam is essentially and fundamentally a religion of moderation; its epistemology is neither exclusively rationalist, nor empiricist, nor intuitionist. It employs all the sources of knowledge – reason, sense–experience and intuition – to arrive at the knowledge of truth, and integrates the relative truth supplied by them with the absolute truth revealed by God to the Prophet Muhammad. In Islam and the civilisation which it created there was a veritable celebration of knowledge, all of whose forms were, in one way or another, related to the sacred, extending in a hierarchy from an 'empirical' and rational mode of knowing to that highest form of knowledge (*al-ma'rifah* or *'irfan*). In other words, Islamic epistemology is an integrated whole of rationalism, empiricism and intuitionism, under the overriding authority of the knowledge revealed by God to the Prophet. In Islam, reason and experience are valid channels by which knowledge is attained – knowledge, that is, at the rational and empirical level of normal experience. We maintain that there is another level; but even at this other, spiritual level, reason and experience are still valid, only that they are of a transcendental order. 'In order to attain a true and comprehensive knowledge we must integrate the findings of reason, sense–perception, intuition and revelation into a well-knit whole.' Indeed, 'the Qur'an (41:53; 51:21) regards both *anfus* (subjective, experiential, transcendental knowledge) and *afaq* (objective, empirical, scientific knowledge) as the veritable sources of human knowledge' (Siddiqui, 2003:6; Nasr, 1981:12; al-Attas, 1985:155).

However knowledge is regarded as very important in the Qur'an: it seldom speaks of *kitab* (revealed knowledge) alone, but pairs this with *hikmah* (wisdom) (see 1:129; 3:164). The book gives us knowledge of the true objective of the creation of man. Wisdom makes us realise the rationale, value and importance of this knowledge for ordering our life, individual and collective, in accordance with it. This consists in reflecting on what we already know, and implies extension in depth, in internalising knowledge, rather than in extending the frontiers of knowledge. From the Islamic perspective, all wisdom is at the same time knowledge, but all knowledge is not wisdom. This gives knowledge an edge over wisdom, but it is wisdom, not mere knowledge, which has sole value in the eyes of God. 'Whosoever is given wisdom, is given abundant good' (2:269), says the Qur'an.

For most of the medieval Muslim philosophers, too, wisdom has been related both to knowledge and philosophy and to religion and morality. For example, Ibn Rushd tried to substantiate a cultural vision of wisdom so that it could be acceptable both in the tradition of Islam (religion) and in the tradition of logic (philosophy), thereby removing a possible contradiction between faith and proof (reason). He aspired to consider the rational scope of Islamic culture as a necessary condition of ideal moderation. He regarded this as a method of overcoming sectarianism and dogmatism, lies and defects, and establishing a rich unity of truth and virtuousness. For him, this was an historical-cultural form of mastering the various attempts and possibilities of the synthesis of reason and wisdom, development of rational wisdom and wise rationalism, which, in turn, were nothing else but the wholeness of the moral spirit or monism (al-Janabi, 2002:252).

The dialogue between knowledge and wisdom has broken off in modern times both in the Western world and in the Islamic world. But their preferences have been different; one has preferred knowledge and neglected wisdom, and the other has done the reverse.

As modern Western philosophy has developed since Descartes, 'the connection of philosophy to morality and its accompanying concern with self-knowledge have been set aside. Philosophy as the love of wisdom that considers the true to be the whole has been replaced by the pursuit of method and the truth of the part. The Renaissance humanists' attempt to discover the connections among wisdom, eloquence, and prudence has been given up. In regard to the Socratic tradition of self-knowledge and the humanist tradition of seeking to form thought and human action as "wisdom speaking", philosophy has lost its way' (Verene, 1997:ix). In the end, knowledge without wisdom has made modern man spiritually homeless, alien to himself or herself, and has challenged humanity and the earth with many global cultural, ethical and environmental crises. Rationalist and positivist epistemology followed by an atheist and naturalist ontology and by relativist and nihilist ethics have really brought more knowledge to the modern world but probably less wisdom, more power but less virtue, and more pleasure but less peace.

In the seventeenth century, the contemporary philosopher of Descartes (1596–1650) in Islamic World was Sadr al-Din al-Shirazi (also known as Mulla Sadra, 1571–1640) and, in comparison to Descartes, his preference tended towards the side of wisdom rather than knowledge. One of his major philosophical works is *Transcendental Wisdom*, better known as *The Four Journeys* (*al-Asfar al-Arba'ah*). Roughly after Mulla Sadra's lifetime, the dialogue and balance of knowledge and wisdom could not have been maintained in the Islamic world as well. The spirit of the last centuries in the Islamic world has been mainly mystical rather than rationalistic or balanced, and many people have acquired practical wisdom enough for living a good life. As Iqbal said, 'The more genuine schools of Sufism have, no doubt, done good work in shaping and directing the evolution of religious exper-ience in Islam; but their latter-day representatives, owing to their ignorance of the modern mind, have become absolutely incapable of receiving any fresh inspiration from modern thought and experience' (1988:v). At the end, wisdom without knowledge has made Muslim man and woman materially homeless, scientifically and technologically backwards and culturally fragile. Mystical and practical wisdom followed by an idealist ontology and univer-salist ethics brought to the Muslim world more wisdom but less knowledge, more virtue but less power, and more internal peace but less international prestige.

Neither the Western nor the Islamic world, which brought off the dialogue of the accompanying and complementary concepts of knowledge and wisdom for three centuries, could have escaped from various crises and they could not have arrived at a more ideal situation. Muslim intellectuals (the modernists and some others) became aware of the crisis in their world in the late nineteenth century; and Western intellectuals (the postmodernists and some others) became aware of their crisis in the late twentieth century. But, in our view, the search for solutions does not give much hope to either world; because the solutions are too simple, that is, they suggest rejecting the past approach completely and give excessive emphasis to the other extreme edge of the dichotomy. For most of the postmodernists (Westerners or Muslim alike), such concepts as foundation, knowledge, reason, rationality, reality, truth, objectivity, science, universal values and virtues are taboo and reactionary concepts; everything is relative and anything goes. For most of the modernists, too, such concepts as wisdom, heart, spirituality, goodness, subjectivity, belief, faith, traditional values and virtues are almost taboo and reactionary concepts. For them, everything is dependent on science and reason, and nothing is allowed without their permission.

A better way to solve the epistemological crises and to promote overall development seems to be to reinstate the dialogue between knowledge and wisdom. There should be a close relationship between all kinds of knowledge and human discourse and action, and knowledge should have the quality of being a guide to life and of finding a meaning in life. Knowledge of the self or subjective knowledge should also be considered as a source and criteria of knowledge; and development of the self and of the human condition in general should be considered one of the main goals of acquiring knowledge.

There is no need to waste more time on the alternative and exclusivist extreme edges of modern and postmodern epistemological dichotomies, such as objectivism, relativism and the others, in any part of the world. Knowledge which is not complemented by wise action is insufficient to prevent or lessen the sufferings of individuals and to promote their self-knowledge, self-realisation and virtuous happiness. In the same way, practical wisdom or just free action that is not originated and supported by firm knowledge is not secure and sound enough for the same purpose, either. So, we should try to develop a 'sophialogical' (from 'sophia' and logical) epistemology and world-view which has a global and perennial foundation in all the great cultures, civilisations and religions of the world. Only in such a case can we make the two most beautiful wishes in complete sincerity, for the whole of humanity: tomorrow let there be fewer things we do not know, and let there be less evil and suffering we cannot prevent.

This sort of complementary and holistic approach is really needed to ensure dialogic and peaceful relations amongst Muslims and non-Muslims. It is also completely in accordance with the key characteristics of Muslims, namely, a moderate or 'well-balanced middle nation' to be witnesses for mankind (Qur'an, 2:147), and with the basic motto and mentality of Islam, 'both–and', in balance, harmony and equilibrium. As a result, the optimistic future of Muslims is founded on how they will fulfil their role as the 'middle nation' and how they will understand and succeed in the best-known prayer taught in the Qur'an, 'Lord! Give us what is good in this world and in the Hereafter' (2:201).

Bibliography

Abduh, Muhammad (1966) *The Theology of Unity*, tr. Ishaq Musa'ad and Kenneth Cragg, London: George Allen & Unwin Ltd.

Affifi, A.E. (1964) *The Mystical Philosophy of Muhyiddin Ibnu'l Arabi*, Cambridge: Cambridge University Press.

Ahmed, Akbar S. (1988) *Discovering Islam: Making Sense of Muslim History and Society*, Lahore: Vanguard.

Ahmed, Akbar S. (1992) *Postmodernism and Islam: Predicament and Promise*, London and New York: Routledge.

Ahmed, Akbar S. (2003) *Islam Under Siege: Living Dangerously in a Post-honor World*, Cambridge: Polity Press.

Ahmed, Akbar S. and Hastings Donnan (eds.) (1994) *Islam, Globalization and Postmodernity*, London and New York: Routledge.

Ali, A.K.M. Ayyub (1963) 'Maturidism', in M.M. Sharif (ed.), *A History of Muslim Philosophy*, vol. 1, Wiesbaden: Otto Harrossowitz.

Ansari, Muhammad Abdul Haq (1986) *Sufism and Shari'ah: A Study of Shaykh Ahmad Sirhindi's Effort to Reform Sufism*, Leicester: The Islamic Foundation.

Arkoun, Mohammed (1994) *Rethinking Islam: Common Questions, Uncommon Answers*, tr. and ed. Robert D. Lee, Oxford: Westview Press.

Ates, Suleyman (1999–2000) 'The Attitude of the Koran Towards the Divine religions', *Kur'an Mesaji*, year 2, nos. 22, 23, 24.

al-Attas, S. M. Naquib (1985) *Islam, Secularism and the Philosophy of the Future,* London, New York: Mansell Publishing Limited.

Aydin, Mehmet S. (1987) *Din Felsefesi* [*The Philosophy of Religion*, in Turkish], 3rd edn, Ankara: Selcuk Yayinlari.

Badham, Paul (1998) *The Contemporary Challenge of Modernist Theology*, Cardiff: University of Wales Press.

Baldick, Julian (1989) *Mystical Islam: An Introduction to Sufism,* London: I.B.Tauris.

Barbour, Ian (2000) *When Science Meets Religion*, London: SPCK.

Bayrakdar, Mehmet (1987) *Islam'da Evrimci Yaratilis Teorisi* [*Evolutionist Theory of Creation in Islam*, in Turkish], Istanbul: Insan Yayinlari.

Brohi, Allahbukhsh K. (1988) 'The Qur'an and Its Impact on Human History', in Khurshid Ahmad (ed.) *Islam: Its Meaning and Message*, Leicester: The Islamic Foundation.

al-Bukhari, Abu Abdullah Muhammad b. Ismail (1987) *Sahih al-Bukhari*, Beirut: Dar al-Kalem.

Capan, Ergun (ed.) (2004) *Terror and Suicide Attacks: An Islamic Perspective*,

New Jersey: The Light, Inc.

Chittick, William C. (1995) 'Sufism', in *The Oxford Encyclopedia of the Modern Islamic World*, John L. Esposito, Editor-in-chief, vol. 4., New York, Oxford: Oxford University Press.

Chittick, William (2003) *Sufism: A Short Introduction*, Oxford: Oneworld Publications.

Chittick, William C. and Sachiko Murata (1994) *The Vision of Islam*, New York: Paragon House.

Coward, Harold (2000) *Pluralism in the World Religions: A Short Introduction*, Oxford: Oneworld.

Cragg, Kenneth (1969) *The House of Islam*, Belmond, California: Dickenson Publishing Company.

Craig, William Lane (1979) *The Kalam Cosmological Argument*, London and Basingstoke: Macmillan.

Davidson, Herbert A. (1987) *Proofs for Eternity, Creation and the Existence of God in Medieval Islamic and Jewish Philosophy*, New York and Oxford: Oxford University Press.

Dawkins, Richard (1991) *The Blind Watchmaker* [1986], London: Penguin Books.

De Boer, T.J. (1981) 'Ethics and Morality (Muslim)', in *Encyclopedia of Religion and Ethics*, ed. James Hasting, Edinburgh: T. & T. Clark.

Denny, Frederick Mathewson (1994) *An Introduction to Islam*, New York: Macmillan Publishing Company.

Ernst, Carl W. (2003) *Following Muhammad: Rethinking Islam in the Contemporary World*, Chapel Hill & London: The University of North Carolina Press.

Esposito, John L. (1991) *Islam: The Straight Path*, New York, Oxford: Oxford University Press.

Esposito, John L. (1992) *The Islamic Threat: Myth or Reality?* New York, Oxford: Oxford University Press.

Esposito, John L. (1995) 'Islam', in *The Oxford Encyclopedia of the Modern Islamic World*, John L. Esposito, Editor-in-chief, vol. 2, New York, Oxford: Oxford University Press.

Fakhry, Majid (1997) *A Short Introduction to Islamic Philosophy, Theology and Mysticism*, Oxford: Oneworld Publications.

al-Faruqi, Isma'il R. and Lois Lamya' al-Faruqi (1986) *The Cultural Atlas of Islam*, New York: Macmillan Publishing Company.

Flew, Antony (ed.) (1979) *A Dictionary of Philosophy*, London: Pan Books.

Fuller, Graham E. (2003) *The Future of Political Islam*, New York: Palgrave Macmillan.

Gauhar, Altaf (ed.) (1978) *The Challenge of Islam*, London: Islamic Council of Europe.

Gerholm, Thomas (1994) 'Two Muslim Intellectuals in the Postmodern West', in Akbar S. Ahmed and Hastings Donnan (eds.) *Islam, Globalization and Postmodernity*, London and New York: Routledge.

al-Ghazali, Abu Hamid Muhammad (n.d.) *Ihya Ulum ad-Din*, Beirut, Lebanon:

Dar al-Qalem.

al-Ghazali, Abu Hamid Muhammad (1953) *The Faith and Practice of al-Ghazali [Deliverance from Error],* tr. W. Montgomery Watt, London: George Allen and Unwin.

al-Ghazali, Abu Hamid Muhammad (1987) al-Hikma fi Mahlugat Allah, Beirut: al-Kutub al-Sagafiyya.

Halman, Talat S. (ed.) (1991) *Yunus Emre and His Mystical Poetry*, Bloomington, Indiana: Indiana University Turkish Studies.

Hamidullah, Muhammad (1980) *Introduction to Islam*, Paris: Centre Culturel Islamique.

Haneef, Suzanne (n.d.) *What Everyone Should Know About Islam and Muslims*, Lahore: Kazi Publications.

Hassan, Riffat (2006) 'Are Human Rights Compatible with Islam? The Issue of the Rights of Women in Muslim Communities', www.religiousconsultation. org/hassan2.htm [Accessed November 2006].

Hick, John (1970) *Arguments for the Existence of God*, London: Macmillan.

Hick, John (1980) 'Whatever Path Men Choose is Mine', in John Hick and Brian Hebblethwaite (eds.) *Christianity and Other Religions*, Glasgow: Fount.

Hick, John (1987) 'Religious Pluralism,' in *The Encyclopedia of Religion*, ed. Mircea Eliade, New York: Macmillan Publishing Company; London: Collier Macmillan.

Hick, John (1988) *God and the Universe of Faith: Essays in the Philosophy of Religion*, London: Macmillan.

Hick, John H. (1990) *Philosophy of Religion*, New Jersey: Prentice Hall, Englewood Cliffs.

The Holy Qur'an with English Translation (1996) The Translation Committee, Istanbul: İlmi Neşriyat.

The Holy Qur'an: English Translation of the Meanings and Commentary (1410 H) Revised & edited by the Presidency of Islamic Researches, IFTA, call and guidance, al-Medina al-Munawarah: King Fahd Holy Qur'an Printing Complex.

Hoodbhoy, Pervez (1991) *Islam and Science: Religious Orthodoxy and the Battle for Rationality*, London and New Jersey: Zed Books Ltd.

Hoodbhoy Pervez (1995) 'Science', in *The Oxford Encyclopedia of the Modern Islamic World*, John L. Esposito, Editor-in-chief, vol. 4, New York, Oxford: Oxford University Press.

Ibn Khaldun (1958) *The Muqaddimah: An Introduction to History*, tr. Franz Rosenthal, vol. 3, London: Routledge & Kegan Paul.

Ibn Rushd, Abu'l Walid (1961) *Averroes on the Harmony of Religion and Philosophy*, tr. and introduction by G. Hourani, London: Luzac.

Ibn Rushd, Abu'l Walid (1969) *Averroes'* Tahafut al-Tahafut (The Incoherence of the Incoherence) tr. Simon Van Den Bergh, vol. 1, London: Luzac & Company Ltd.

Iqbal, Afzal (1983) *The Life and Work of Jalal-ud-din Rami,* London: The Octagon Press.

Iqbal, Mohammad (1988) *The Reconstruction of Religious Thought in Islam,*

Lahore: M. Ashraf.

Izetbegovic, 'Aliya 'Ali (1991) *Islam Between East and West*, Indianapolis, Indiana: American Trust Publications.

Izutsu, Toshihiko (1980) *The Concept of Belief in Islamic Theology: A Semantic Analysis of Iman and Islam* [1965], New York: Books for Libraries, a Division of Arno Press.

al-Janabi, Maitham (2002) 'Islamic Culture as Search of a Golden Mean', in Nur Kirabaev, Yuriy Pochta (eds.) *Values in Islamic Culture and the Experience of History*, Washington, D.C.: The Council for Research in Values and Philosophy.

al-Jawzıyyah, Ibn Qayyım (n.d.) *al-Ruh*, Cairo: Dar al-Nehr al-Nil.

Kahveci, Niyazi (1993) *The Basics of Islam*, Ankara: Turkish Religious Foundation.

al-Kalabadhi, Abu Bakr (1979) *The Doctrine of the Sufis (Kitab al-ta'aaruf li-madhhab ahl al-tasawwuf)*, tr. A. J. Arberry, Cambridge: Cambridge University Press.

Khan, Muhammad Zafrulla (1962) *Islam: Its Meaning for Modern Man,* London: Routledge and Kegan Paul.

Martin, Richard C. (1996) *Islamic Studies: A History of Religions Approach*, New Jersey: Prentice Hall.

Matson, Wallace I. (1965) *The Existence of God*, Ithaca, New York: Cornell University Press.

McDermott, Mustafa Yusuf, Muhammad Manazır Ahsan (1986) *The Muslim Guide*, Leicester: The Islamic Foundation.

Muslim, Ibn Al-Hajjaj Al-Qushayri (1972) *Sahih Muslim: Being Traditions of the sayings and doings of the Prophet Muhammad. Rendered into English by 'Abdul Hamid Siddiqi*, Lahore: Muhammed Ashraf.

Muwahidi, Ahmad Anisuzzaman (1989) 'Islamic Perspectives on Death and Dying', in A. Berger, P. Badham, A. H. Kutscher, J. Berger, M. Perry, J. Beloff (eds.) *Perspectives on Death and Dying: Cross-Cultural and Multi-Disciplinary Views*, Philadelphia: The Charles Press, Publishers.

Nasr, Seyyed Hossein (1963) 'Fakhr al-Din Razi', in M.M. Sharif (ed.) *A History of Muslim Philosophy*, vol. 1, Wiesbaden: Otto Harrossowitz.

Nasr, Seyyed Hossein (1976) 'The Western World and Its Challenges to Islam', in Khurshid Ahmad (ed.) *Islam: Its Meaning and Message*, 2nd edn, Leicester: The Islamic Foundation.

Nasr, Seyyed Hossein (1981) *Knowledge and the Sacred,* New York: Crossroad.

Nasr, Seyyed Hossein (1991) *Sufi Essays*, Albany: State University of New York Press.

Nasr, Seyyed Hossein (2002) *The Heart of Islam: Enduring Values for Humanity*, New York: HarperSanFrancisco.

Nyang, Sulayman (1987) 'The Teaching of the Quran Concerning Life after Death', in P. Badham and L. Badham (eds.) *Death and Immortality in the Religions of the World*, New York: Paragon House.

Peterson, Michael, William Hasker, Bruce Reichenbach, David Basinger (1991)

Reason and Religious Belief: An Introduction to the Philosophy of Religion, Oxford and New York: Oxford University Press.

Plantinga, Alvin (2000) *Warranted Christian Belief*, Oxford and New York: Oxford University Press.

Qadir, C.A. (1988) *Philosophy and Science in the Islamic World*, London, New York: Croom Helm.

al-Qardawi, Yusuf (1998) 'Extremism', in Charles Kurzman (ed.) *Liberal Islam: A Sourcebook*, New York, Oxford: Oxford University Press.

Qurashi, Mazhar Mahmood (1995) 'Natural Sciences', in *The Oxford Encyclopedia of the Modern Islamic World*, John L. Esposito, Editor-in-chief, New York, Oxford: Oxford University Press.

al-Qurtubi, Abu Abdillah Muhammad b. Ahmad (1991) *al-Tazkirah*, Cairo: Dar al-Deyyan.

Rahman, Fazlur (1952) *Avicenna's Psychology: An English Translation of Kitab al-Najat*, bk II, ch. VI with historico-philosophical notes and textual improvements on the Cairo edition, London: Oxford University Presse.

Rahman, Fazlur (1966), *Islam*, New York, Chicago, San Francisco: Holt, Rinehart and Winston.

al-Razi, Fahruddin (n.d.) *Mefatih al-Gayb*, Istanbul: Şirket-i Sahafiyye-i Osmaniyye.

Reich, Walter (1990) 'Introduction', in Walter Reich (ed.) *Origins of Terrorism: Psychologies, Ideologies, Theologies, States of Mind*, Cambridge: Cambridge University Press.

Rumi, M. Jalalu'l-Din (1950) *Selections from His Writings*, tr. with introduction and notes by Reynold A. Nicholson, London: George Allen and Unwin.

Sajid, Abduljalil (2001) 'Islam against Religious Extremism and Fanaticism', *Dialogue & Alliance*, Winter 2001, vol. 15, no. 2.

Schimmel, Annemarie (1975) *Mystical Dimensions of Islam,* Chapel Hill: The University of North Carolina Press.

Schimmel, Annemarie (2000) 'Reason and Mystical Experience in Sufism', in Farhad Daftary (ed.) *Intellectual traditions in Islam*, London, New York: I.B. Tauris.

Sharif, M.M. (1963) 'Philosophical Teachings of the Qur'an', in M. M. Sharif (ed.) *A History of Muslim Philosophy*, Wiesbaden: Otto Harrassowitz.

Siddiqui, B. H. (09.07.2003), 'Knowledge: An Islamic Perspective' http://www.crvp.org/book/Series02/IIA-3/chapter_x.htm [Accessed November 2006].

Smith, Huston (1996) 'Postmodernism and the World's Religions', in Sharifah Shifa al-Attas (ed.) *Islam and the Challenge of Modernity: Historical and Contemporary Contexts*, Kuala Lumpur: ISTAC.

Smith, Jane Idleman and Yvonne Y. Haddad (1981) *The Islamic Understanding of Death and Resurrection*, Albany, N.Y.: State University of New York Press.

Swinburne, Richard G. (1996) *Is There a God?*, Oxford and New York: Oxford University Press.

Verene, Donald Phillip (1997) *Philosophy and the Return to Self-Knowledge*, New Haven and London: Yale University Press.

Waines, David (1996) *An Introduction to Islam*, Cambridge: Cambridge University Press.

Walzer, R. (1960) 'Akhlak', in *The Encyclopaedia of Islam*, new edn, Leiden: E. J. Brill; London: Luzac & Co.

Watson, Francis M. (1976) *Political Terrorism: The Threat and the Response*, Washington, New York: Robert B. Luce.

Yaran, Cafer S. (2003) *Islamic Thought on the Existence of God: Contributions and Contrasts with Contemporary Western Philosophy of Religion*, Washington, D.C.: The Council for Research in Values and Philosophy.

Yaran, Cafer S. (2004a) *Muslim Religious Experiences*, Lampeter: Religious Experience Research Centre.

Yaran, Cafer S (2004b) 'Religious Culture, Terrorism and Ethnical Peace in the Balkans', in Bogdana Todorova (ed.) *The Balkans as Reality*, Sofia: IPhR-BAS.

Yaran, Cafer S. (2004c) 'Religious Pluralism after Modernity: Towards a Non-Radical Version', in Vladimir Peterca and Magdelena Dumitrana (eds.) *Religion and Culture after Modernity*, Bucharest: Archiepiscopia Romano-Catolica.

Yaran, Cafer S. (2005) 'Wisdom as an Inter-Religious Concept for Peace', in J. D. Woodberry, O. Zumrut and M. Koylu (eds.) *Muslim and Christian Reflections on Peace*, New York, Oxford: University Press of America.

Yaran, Cafer S. and Sinasi Gunduz (eds.) (2005) *Change and Essence: Dialectical Relations Between Change and Continuity in the Turkish Intellectual Tradition*, Washington, D.C.: The Council for Research in Values and Philosophy.

Zayd, Nasr Abu (2004) 'The Qur'anic Concept of Justice', www.polylog.org/them/2/fcs8-en.htm [Accessed November 2006].

Glossary

Adhaan: the call to prayer.

'Adl: justice; the mean or balance between two extremes.

Akhlak: Islamic morality.

'Alim: a scholar of the religious sciences.

'Amal: act of obedience, good work.

Aya (pl. *ayat*): a single verse in the Qur'an.

Baqa': 'subsistence', the highest station in Sufism.

Bid'ah: 'innovation' in Muslim ritual practice or beliefs.

Caliph: head of the Muslim government after the Prophet Muhammad.

Dhikr: 'remembrance', mentioning the name of Allah.

Din: religion in general.

Fana': 'annihilation' in Allah, one of the highest stations in Sufism.

Faqih: a Muslim jurist.

Fatwa: an authoritative, advisory legal opinion.

Fiqh: the science of Islamic jurisprudence.

Hadith: a report or tradition of the sayings and deeds of the Prophet.

Hajj: pilgrimage to Mecca.

Hal: a spiritual 'state'.

Halal: lawful, allowable.

al-hamdu li'-Llah: 'Praise be to Allah.'

Haram: 'prohibited', 'forbidden' action according to the law.

Hijra: the migration of Muhammad and his companions from Mecca to Medina in 622 CE.

'Ibadah: an act of worship, including prayer, fasting, pilgrimage, etc.

Ihsan: perfection of faith and action; worshipping God as if one sees Him.

Ijma: 'consensus' in Islamic jurisprudence.

Ijtihad: the exercise of independent judgement in Islamic law.

'Ilm: 'knowledge', 'learning', 'science'.

Imam: a leader, especially in prayer.

Iman: faith, belief.

In sha'a Allah: 'If Allah wills.'

Islah: reform.

Islam: recognition of and submission to the command of Allah.

Jami': congregational mosque.

Jinn: invisible, non-human creatures created by God.

Kafir: 'infidel', 'unbeliever'.

Kalam: the discipline of Islamic dialectical theology.

Karamah (pl. *karamat*): 'miracle' attributed to a Muslim saint.

Kufr: unbelief.

Madhab: 'school' of Muslim religious law.

Makruh: 'reprehensible' action.

Mandub: 'commendable' action.

Maqam: 'station' on the Sufi path.

Ma'rifah: gnosis; experiential knowledge of Allah.

Mubah: 'permissible' action.

Mufti: a specialist in Islamic law competent to issue a *fatwa*.

Mu'jizat: 'miracle' attributed to a prophet.

Mu'min: 'believer' in Allah.

Murtadd: an apostate from Islam.

Mushrik: polytheist, idolater.

Nabi: 'prophet'.

Niyyah: intention.

Qadar: the Divine measure or determination of human events.

Qiblah: the direction towards Mecca.

Qiyas: analogy.

Rabb: Lord.

Rasul: 'messenger' of Allah.

Sadaqah: non-obligatory alms.

Sahabah: the companions of the Prophet.

Salat: prayer.

Sawm: fasting.

Shahadah: 'witnessing'.

Shariah: the sacred law.

Shukr: gratitude or thankfulness.

Shura: consultation.

Sufi: a Muslim mystic.

Sunnah: the normative practice of the Prophet.

Surah: a chapter division of the Qur'an.

Tasawwuf: Arabic term for Sufism.

Tawhid: the doctrine of Allah's oneness.

Ummah: the worldwide Muslim community.

Wahy: revelation.

Zahid: an ascetic.

Zakat: obligatory alms.

Index